THE LORD OF THE RINGS

WEAPONS AND WARFARE

Dedicated to the memory of William Alfred Brunger (1912–2003),
a man of peace during times of war

I would gratefully like to acknowledge the assistance of the following people,
without whom this book would not have been possible:
Jeremy Bennett, Hannah Bianchini, Jan Blenkin, Melissa Booth, David Brawn,
Terence Caven, Vicki Connor at Te Papa, Daniel Falconer, Robert Foster, Mike Grealish,
John Howe, Peter Jackson, Jane Johnson, Alan Lee, Christopher Lee, Peter Lyon,
Warren Mahy, Mel Morris, Erin O'Donnell, Trace Owen, Daniel Reeve, Christian Rivers,
Edward Smith, Valerie Smith, Richard Taylor, J.E.A. Tyler, Tony Wolf, Ben Wootten and,
of course, the late Professor J.R.R. Tolkien.
I would additionally like to thank L'Affaire le chat for support (après le déluge viens plus déluge!)
and Lala, Lula and Max for helping to keep my head above water and below the parapets
during the writing of this book. My love to you all.

Library of Congress Cataloging-in-Publication Data is available.
ISBN 0-618-39099-5
ISBN 0-618-39100-2 (pbk.)

Design: Terence Caven
Production: Arjen Jansen
Photography: Pierre Vinet, with Eric Axene, Chris Coad, Ken George, Grant Maiden and
courtesy of New Line Productions, Inc.
Artwork, maps and sculptures: Alan Lee, John Howe, Jeremy Bennett, Jamie Beswarick,
Max Dennison, Yanick Dusseault, Daniel Falconer, Gus Hunter, Roger Kupelian, Paul Lasaine,
Sacha Lees, Warren Mahy, Daniel Reeve, Christian Rivers, Ben Wootten.
Battle plans by Warren Mahy & Ben Wootten; Moria plan by Ben Wootten & Warren Mahy,
based on drawings by Alan Lee.

Printed and bound in Belgium by Proost NV, Turnhout

HC 10 9 8 7 6 5 4 3

THE LORD OF THE RINGS™

WEAPONS AND WARFARE

AN ILLUSTRATED GUIDE TO THE BATTLES, ARMIES AND ARMOR OF MIDDLE-EARTH

CHRIS SMITH

HOUGHTON MIFFLIN COMPANY
BOSTON   NEW YORK   2003

Contents

Foreword

WHEN I WAS A BOY, I was brought up on Grimm's *Fairy Tales*, *Gulliver's Travels*, *Alice in Wonderland* and *Through the Looking Glass*. I thought these books were weird, fascinating and enthralling. Many generations have felt the same way.

As a teenager and a classical scholar, I was totally involved in the works of the Greek and Latin poets and dramatists, particularly Homer's *Iliad* and *Odyssey*, which I learned in the original language. I was completely fascinated by these great epics of battle, heroism, treachery and doom. I had always been fascinated by myth and legend, and I was soon immersed in the Icelandic Sagas, together with Norse and Celtic mythology, about which I learned a great deal. Pure coincidence in view of what was to come many years later.

Until I "discovered" Tolkien, my favorite book had always been *The Sword in the Stone* by T.H. White. I still have all his books.

Then came *The Hobbit*. An entirely new world opened itself to me. I was and am totally captivated. But this was the prelude to a story in three acts as it were: *The Lord of the Rings*. By the time I had read all three books, I knew beyond any doubt that I had been taken into a world of magic and enchantment unlike any literary work I had ever explored. What Professor Tolkien achieved is unique in the literature of my lifetime. Indeed, in my opinion, he had reached the peak of literary invention of all time. Nothing like it has ever existed, and probably never will.

To have been involved in bringing this epic to the screen has been a privilege and an honor for us all, and the resulting worldwide acclamation will continue as long as the cinema exists. Motion picture history has been made that will never be surpassed.

Much of the military detail and history of the three films has been captured in *The Lord of the Rings: Weapons & Warfare*, and readers of this book will be able to gain valuable further insight into the history of the War of the Ring.

The Return of the King is the logical conclusion of the trilogy. It is full of beauty, heroism, courage, darkness and doom, mounting to the final glory of the triumph of good over evil. The spirit of Tolkien will continue to amaze and delight many millions all over the world. I am but one of those enchanted by its magic. It is sublime – a true saga.

Christopher Lee
Wellington, New Zealand
July 2003

Introduction

MIDDLE-EARTH WAS A LAND OF CONFLICT. In every sense, it was a world shaped and defined by the eternal struggle between good and evil. Its mountains, seas, cities and plains were literally carved by eons of war between these opposing forces, and every race or culture that inhabited the world was characterized by the part it played. Each was an embodiment of some element of the battle of ideologies that had wrought and unmade Middle-earth time and again over the ages.

Men, of all the races of Middle-earth, were closest in spirit to the center of the conflict, for Men possessed the greatest predisposition toward acts of greatness and, at the same time, those of darkness. Men's hearts were fickle and fragile things. The wills of Men could be swayed by pride, vengeance, greed and love. For Men the wars of Middle-earth were not for land or power so much as for redemption. They sought to rise above themselves, to conquer their own base nature and prove themselves to be something greater and nobler, above temptation and human weakness.

Time and again Men failed before the face of temptation, but time and again they crawled back to redeem themselves with acts of valor and purity of heart. So it was with Isildur at Orodruin, who succumbed to the lure of the Ring, only to be succeeded by Aragorn, who restored the pride of Gondor. So it was also with Boromir, who fell into evil but was saved by his valor before the end. Men fought to prove themselves worthy of their honor and to conquer not only the evil without but that which lay within.

For Elves, the wars of Middle-earth were different. The Elves were perhaps the closest of all races to being incorruptible, though even they could fall. When Elves fought, it was with sadness and regret, for their nature impelled them to acts of nobility and gentleness. They were creators and artists before they were warriors.

The Elves of the Third Age fought to leave behind a better world for the younger races. For thousands of years they had dwelt in Middle-earth and fought the darkness, and yet still it remained. Recognizing the waning of their age, the Elves fought to give some meaning to their legacy in Middle-earth – a final gift to those that would follow. It pained them to fight, for their hearts hearkened to the values of the distant West, a place where evil held no sway.

For the Orcs, who were in every way the opposite of Elves, war was their nature. Brutal, ugly creatures, the Orcs fought because they knew no other existence. Once Elves, they had been corrupted and poisoned against their own nature and were perpetually in conflict with themselves; thus they knew no rest or comfort except in battle.

Finally, there were the hobbits, who held the fate of all Middle-earth in their tiny hands. How ironic that in all the great battles and tribulations of the world, to those for whom conflict was most alien should fall the task of ending all conflict forever. Hobbits represented the awakening new world, the innocent new life that gives of itself to redeem and save everyone else. The sacrifice of that innocence was the greatest gift the hobbits ever gave to the peoples of Middle-earth, and it saved them all.

Daniel Falconer and Richard Taylor
Wellington, New Zealand, July 2003

The History of the War of the Ring

LONG LONG AGO, some 5,000 years before the Fellowship was formed to escort the Ring-bearer, Frodo Baggins of the Shire, to the land of Mordor, the Dark Lord Sauron sought the friendship of the Elves. At this time Sauron was still able to assume fair form and in this guise he came to the Elves of Eregion, the realm that lay close to the West-gate of Moria; seeking knowledge, the Elves welcomed him, and together they fashioned the Rings of Power, but ever was treachery in his heart and Sauron longed only to subjugate all the peoples of Middle-earth.

Returning to Mordor, he secretly made the One Ring, pouring his malice, his cruelty, and his will to dominate into it so that it would be the ruler of all the other Rings. But because the Elven-rings were artifacts of great magic, Sauron needed to pour much of his power into the One so that he could have the mastery of them. During this time, and without Sauron's help,

A map of southern Arnor, Eriador and the Misty Mountains, c. Second Age, believed to be a Númenórean translation of an Elven original.

I

Eriador, looking east to the Misty Mountains.

Celebrimbor alone made the three Greatest Rings – Vilya, the Ring of Air and greatest of the three, Nenya, the Ring of Water, and Narya, the Ring of Fire – and these were given to Gil-galad, High-king of the Noldor, Galadriel, Queen of Lothlórien, and Círdan of the Grey Havens.

However, as soon as Sauron put on the Ring his intentions were perceived by the Elves. Furious at this discovery, Sauron launched a terrible war upon them; his army of Orcs and other beasts swept over the Misty Mountains, killing as they moved west, covering all the lands in darkness. The Elves were only saved from annihilation by the arrival of a huge fleet of Númenórean men; such was their power in arms that Sauron's Orcs were utterly defeated, leaving him with nothing but his personal bodyguard, who were driven back into Mordor. This humiliation earned them the eternal hatred of the Dark Lord, who would never rest until he had destroyed every last descendant of Númenor.

After this, Gil-galad, Galadriel, and Círdan never openly displayed their Rings again, although their power was ever at work, strengthening and enriching the realms of Lindon, Lórien and the Grey Havens.

During these dark years Sauron captured all of the Rings of Power, save those belonging to the three Elves. Seven he gave to the Dwarf-lords, and nine he gave to Kings of Men. Upon each Dwarf-ring a magnificent treasure hoard was founded, and each of the Kings of Men became powerful beyond measure. But the malevolent control that the One Ring exerted over these Rings and their wearers could not be undone. Although the Dwarves were resistant to Sauron's domination, their treasure hoards were cursed and each was consumed in dragon-fire. But where the Dwarves were strong in spirit the men were weak, and they could not escape the dominion of the Dark Lord – these proud rulers would become slaves, and their once-golden lives would decay into an endless torment of shadow and suffering.

For over a thousand years Middle-earth had peace, although the malice of Sauron was ever at work. His greatest achievement in

ABOVE *Replicas of the three Elven-rings, Vilya, Nenya and Narya.*
RIGHT *Sauron's Orcs sweep west into Eriador.*

The Elven realm of Lothlórien, with the Great Tree at Caras Galadhon clearly visible.

those years was allowing himself to be captured and taken to the island of Númenor, where he managed to corrupt the proud and fearless Númenóreans who lived there and bring about the downfall and complete destruction of their realm.

The survivors of this cataclysm settled in Middle-earth, building the great cities of Osgiliath and Minas Anor and Minas Ithil in the kingdom of Gondor. Sauron himself was destroyed during the downfall but his spirit returned to Mordor, although it was many years before he could take physical form again. Seeing how much the men had already achieved during his absence, Sauron began to rebuild his own forces, and quickly he launched an attack on Gondor, hoping to crush the fledgling kingdom before it could become

a threat. Minas Ithil was captured, and would ever after be known as Minas Morgul, but Isildur managed to escape down the River Anduin, sailing north to Elendil's kingdom of Arnor to raise the alarm. Led by Isildur's brother, Anárion, the remaining Gondorians stemmed the tide of attack, holding the line at Osgiliath, but they were now all too aware that it would not be the last. Seeing that the danger from Sauron's army would continue to grow with every passing year, Elendil and Gil-galad joined in league, agreeing to launch a final, do-or-die attack upon the Dark Lord, one last throw of the dice to end his tyranny: this union would be known as the Last Alliance of Elves and Men.

RIGHT *Replicas of the seven Dwarven-rings.*
BELOW *The nine Kings of Men receive their Rings.*

The Last Alliance of Elves and Men

BECAUSE ELENDIL AND GIL-GALAD had taken the initiative, they had the luxury of time to prepare for this battle. Both kings spent two years gathering their forces; Elendil and Isildur met Gil-galad at the watchtower of Amon Sûl on Weathertop and together they led their hosts to Rivendell, where they were joined by Elrond and his company of Elves. In Rivendell they spent a further three years forging swords and armor and making spears and shields with which to arm themselves. Climbing over the Misty Mountains, they journeyed south down the River Anduin, gathering Elves from Greenwood and Lórien, and eventually were joined by the army of Númenóreans from Gondor led by Isildur's brother Anárion. The host that comprised this Last Alliance of Elves and Men is said to have been the greatest seen in Middle-earth since the beginning of the First Age: ten times ten thousand strong.

Together, the two forces marched across the stony Dagorlad Plain, intending to carry on to the Barad-dûr itself, but a massive army of Sauron's Orcs (some accounts say as many as 500,000) poured through the Black Gates to meet them. Although the Alliance had been marching for several weeks across many leagues, the Elves and Men were ready to face

Elven spearmen advance through the treacherous gloom of the Dagorlad Plain.

ARMOR

Like most Dwarven-made artifacts, Gimli's war gear was extremely well made and left virtually no weak points exposed in its defense. The Dwarves had been making armor for millennia and so knew very well how to protect themselves from swift attacks while they prepared themselves to launch a devastating blow of their own. As a first cushioning layer Gimli would probably have had soft, loose-fitting woolen hose and shirt; a wide leather collar would have gone around the neck, to which were attached sleeves of mail extending to the wrist. This mail was unique to Gimli, as it consisted of flattened rings held together with hexagonal links of fine gold wire. Over these he would have worn long leather gauntlets and boiled leather vambraces with an additional plate laced to the hands, which protected the knuckles (*left*). His arms were further protected by boiled leather pauldrons and rerebraces (*right*) etched and gilded in gold; over his leather boots were attached shinguards of the same boiled leather. To protect the legs, he wore a full skirt of the same special mail, which would probably have been belted to his waist, rather than attached to a tunic, because of its weight. The next layer was a red woolen mantle that was edged in leather and reinforced around the torso, shoulders and back with heavily etched sashes of interlacing leather. Last came the harness: a wide leather belt with a metal buckle decorated in gold held all of the axes except Gimli's battle axe, which was carried from a padded ring set in the back of a bandolier that crisscrossed his shoulders and was attached to the belt. At the back of this were two small pouches that contained his sharpening and repair kits and his meager travel supplies. A bedroll and blanket were carried across his shoulders: in addition to being the best place for keeping it out of the way when he was swinging an axe, it protected his head from the blade of the battle axe. For all the layers and finery of his armor, Gimli's helmet was the most important and heavily worked feature of his outfit. Built around a skull of boiled

leather, the helmet had a leather skirt to which were attached small plates of interlinked mail that formed an aventail protecting all of the neck; inside the skull was a dual layer of a leather coif that was insulated from the helmet by a buffer of stuffed canvas or wool, which would have prevented any impact being transferred to Gimli's head. Around the skull of the helmet was riveted a beautiful steel frame to which were attached cheek-guards: both of these were decorated with a stylized star motif in reference to his name, which means "star" in Khuzdul. The thick, angular frame protected the top of the head by forming a cross, and at the center of this was a circle of onyx: a scarce substance in those days, and one that would have signified great wealth in the owner. With all of this protection, it would have taken a furious and determined assault to get through Gimli's defenses; the only one to achieve this during all the long battles of the War of the Ring was Galadriel, who succeeded in breaking through the barriers of his pride and mistrust and stealing his heart.

The Cave Troll

THE CAVE TROLL ENCOUNTERED by the Fellowship in Moria was one of several species of troll found in Middle-earth during the Second and Third Ages. Others recorded in the Red Book by Bilbo and Frodo are stone trolls, found in the north of Middle-earth, and mountain trolls, which lurked in the mountains of Mordor. Most trolls were evil but stupid, stood twice the height of men, and were very strong. If attacked, they would fight until the death. As the name suggests, cave trolls lived underground and in the dark. If exposed to sunlight they would turn to stone, and even normal interior light would form a scaly crust on their skins, especially if they were hibernating.

It seems quite possible that the cave troll that attacked the Fellowship had been caught and shackled by Moria Orcs while hibernating, and had been used more as a weapon against the Dwarves than as part of the Orc company.

Cave trolls relied more upon their sense of smell than their sight, attacking only what was in their immediate vicinity. When enraged, they made little distinction over whom to attack and so proved unreliable allies when fighting in close quarters. Their tough hides made them difficult to kill, but a well-placed shot at the softer tissues of the throat and mouth could, with luck, find its way through to the tiny brain.

ABOVE *Pencil study of the three stone trolls that still stand in Trollshaw woods.*
RIGHT *Cave-troll sculpture, possibly Third Age Gondorian.*
BELOW *Anatomical studies of a troll found in Minas Tirith archive.*

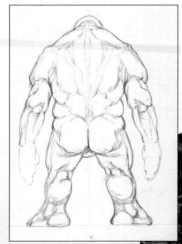

CLUB

A cave troll would often use a weapon when attacking, but because of its low intelligence that weapon was rarely more sophisticated than a club. However, when coupled with its brute strength, this would prove extremely effective.

SPEAR

In its blind desire to get at Frodo and the Ring, which it could feel pushing at its dim intelligence, the cave troll grabbed a discarded Dwarven spear from the floor of the Chamber of Mazarbul and used it to stab Frodo. Down the length of the spear's haft on alternating sides was written in Khuzdul, the language of the Dwarves:

Tarâg-udrig Rakhâs-udrig
Troll-bane Orc-bane

Little is known of the Dwarven language, but it can be seen that the word "Tarâg" is very close to the Sindarin "torog," so it seems fair to assume that one begat the other. Trolls were evidently a menace to both races.

The Orcs of Moria

W HEN THE PITS OF ANGBAND were opened and Morgoth taken away in chains, those of his Orcs who survived the devastation fled to the mountains and dark places of Middle-earth. At this time Dwarves were still populous and lived in the hills of the north, so these renegade Orcs traveled south to the first sanctuary they could find: the Misty Mountains. Here they hid themselves from the light of the sun, and discovery, and established a vast system of underground caves and tunnels. The population was so great that they even had a city, Gundabad, from where these "Goblins" would strike out on sorties, waylaying travelers in Eregion and the Vale of Anduin, and living off their supplies, their horses and the travelers themselves.

Bred in darkness, Orcs naturally shunned the light of day, for they were weakened by the sun's power and blinded by its light. They would venture out in daylight only if coerced or threatened, or when pursuing a particularly hateful enemy; for these occasions, many Orcs had helmets that slotted down over the eyes to reduce the light coming in. When the surviving members of the

ABOVE *Artist's impression of Goblins in Gundabad.*
LEFT *Moria Orcs lived at the tops of the immense Dwarrowdelf pillars.*
BELOW *The subterranean environment caused the Orcs' appearance to change over the centuries.*

Fellowship left Moria they were pursued by Orcs as far as Lórien itself; it turned out to be an ill-advised sortie, for the Orcs were utterly destroyed by Lórien's Elves, led by Haldir.

In appearance, Orcs were short in stature, around five feet tall, about the height of Dwarves but longer-limbed, in many ways like the mythical apes of Far Harad. Having spent centuries in the dark caves, their skin had paled to a dead gray color and their eyes had grown huge to help them see in the poor light. Their rat-like mouths were full of teeth that were broken but still sharp; their ears were long, looking almost as if they had been melted and stretched. They were like nothing so much as cockroaches, numerous and hard to kill, and largely similar in appearance. Malicious and aggressive, they would attack anything that they came into contact with, unless it was of superior strength or numbers. Individually the Moria Orcs were cowardly, preferring to strike from the safety of darkness; their strength was derived from fighting as a pack.

The millennia of the Second and Third Ages saw their ever-increasing population spread throughout the Misty Mountains, but they were afraid of the great Dwarven kingdom of Khazad-dûm – the axes of the Dwarves were always sharpened and eager for Orc-flesh – and so steered clear of the southern arm of the mountain range. But this all changed when the Balrog was awakened and the Dwarves were driven from their ancestral home. Although the Orcs were fearful of this new creature that had arisen, their curiosity and desire to plunder proved irresistible, and they began to creep into the abandoned kingdom. Soon they flooded in, creating a vast new colony that was eager to take possession of all the weapons, armor, ore and equipment the Dwarves had left behind.

Yet Moria still had one lord and master, and it is clear that it would have terrified the Orcs

Goblin archers often carried their bows in their hands to protect them from damage.

as much as it did the other races of Middle-earth. It will never be known exactly what the nature of the relationship was between the Balrog and the Orcs, but the large colony in Moria suggests that the Balrog allowed them to share its domain. One theory is that, in the self-contained environment of the underground halls, the primitive intelligence of the Orcs led them to adopt it as a kind of godlike figure, to be feared and venerated in equal measure; this may have created a shamanistic culture under the mountains where ritual sacrifices, perhaps by immolation, were made to the fiery demon-god in exchange for protection, or perhaps just a deferral in their destruction. As with any cult of this nature, the Orcs would have sought to mimic the appearance of their

deity; indeed, clues can be found to support this in their armor, helmets and swords, in which parallels can be found in the scant descriptions of Balrogs that have been recorded throughout the ages. Yet for all this emulation, they were careful to avoid the demon and lived at the tops of the pillars and in the small tunnels under the halls.

The fighting style of the Moria Orcs, when armed with swords, was to keep low to the ground, scuttling toward their enemy. When about to engage, they would use their swords and shields in a windmill motion. The Orc would hide behind the shield and sword-arm guard, then emerge on the attack, using the sword in short stabbing movements, rather like that of a crab's pincers.

ABOVE *Orc swordsmen crouched low to the ground, striking out from behind their large shield.*
RIGHT *The Orcs were able to scuttle up and down the rocky surfaces using their clawed gauntlets and long toes.*

SWORDS

When the Orcs occupied the caverns and halls of Khazad-dûm, there was a large amount of refined metal waiting to be reformed. The Orcs were not artisans, but they did have some skill in working metal, and so would have hammered out armor and weapons that appear ugly to our eyes but were well made, very sharp and perfectly suited to the creatures using them. The shape of their sword would have been influenced by two things: the way that the Orcs would wield it in battle, and their desire to copy the weapon carried by the Balrog. Although seemingly crude and brutal, the three-foot-long sword was an efficient design, incorporating the handgrip and guard into the blade, protecting the sword hand even as it provided an uninterrupted length of blade that could be used to chop down upon their enemy; the sharpened tip allowed the Orcs to stab at their foe and then retreat back behind their large shield, and the pommel had jagged coronels that would have turned it into a brutal clubhead. Although the blade was quite big for a creature of Orc size, it should be remembered that these Orcs were wiry and were able to climb using their own strength quite easily; there was a lot of power in their musculature, so it would have been no problem for them to swing a sword this big with great force.

DAGGERS

Small daggers that were fashioned out of horn have been recovered. Because of the range of other weapons normally carried, these were probably used for stealthy attacks and for cutting apart food prior to eating it. The source of all the Orcs' horn would have been unsuspecting goats climbing on the mountainside.

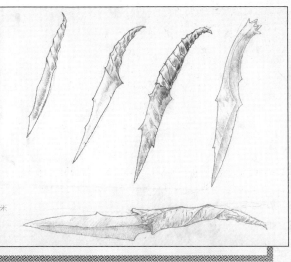

STAFF WEAPONS

There were two types of staff weapon: a spear and a halberd. The spear varied in length between four and five feet and had a barbed metal tip. As with the sword, the Orcs would have ventured out from behind their shields to make short stabbing attacks with it before retreating once again, often using the barb to trip larger opponents. It could also be thrown, but only at a short range: in any case, its relative lightness would have made it largely ineffective against a well-armored Dwarf. The halberd featured what was probably a recycled Dwarven axe blade that had been adapted to the Orcs' design; this would have been more of a threat to their enemies, as its larger and heavier blade would have produced a much more effective striking force. It is assumed that an Orc would have carried either a staff weapon or a sword, as no scabbards, which would have made the carrying of two weapons possible when climbing, have been found.

BOWS

Living under the mountains meant that the Orcs had little wood; there may have been wooden equipment left behind by the Dwarves that could be broken up, but it is likely that the Orcs had to make special sorties to collect wood for kindling and for weapons. Therefore, the bow would have been made almost completely out of horn; it was of a recurved type, shaped so as to get as much power into the short bow as possible. It would have been strung with sinew or twine, although innards could have been used if nothing else was available. In addition to being suited to their relatively short stature, a bow of this size would be easy to carry through the narrow crevices and gloomy corridors without getting hooked up and damaged. A short bow of inferior quality would not have much of a range, but in a darkened environment the line of sight would be poor due to the size of rooms and lack of visibility in the extreme darkness, so the Orcs would not be shooting much beyond 50 yards at a time.

The bows fired small black dartlike arrows, made as quickly and as easily as possible – there would have been a lot of breakage for the same reasons mentioned above, and in any case there would be little chance of recovering them afterward. Accuracy wasn't such an issue across short distances in the dark, and the rock walls would break arrowheads and shafts, so no time was wasted on forging metal heads or fletching with feathers; stone or obsidian and fur or even hair was used instead. (Even on the outside perimeters of Moria the Orcs would have been more likely to catch a mountain goat than a bird, especially as it was usually nighttime when they were abroad.) Again, because of the scarcity of wood, the arrows would have needed to be small, made from wood of whatever quality was available. The Orcs must almost have

been relying on the fact that an arrow would break after one or two shots, so they must have thought of it as a harassing weapon. While it would probably take only one good shot from a longbow to kill someone, it can be imagined that a hunting group of these "Goblins" needed to pepper something with a dozen or so shots before it dropped. Of course, this would have been done from the safety of the upper pillars and walls.

The quiver that carried the arrows was a crude cone of leather, incredibly light and easy to make. It had a long twist of leather up the back so that it could be lashed around the arrows when climbing or traveling at speed. Like most of the equipment carried by the Moria Orcs, it was relatively disposable: when faced with the choice of jettisoning their equipment or falling down an endless chasm, there would be little hesitation.

SHIELDS

The shields were made of metal and were again relatively large. They resembled in shape part of an insect shell or crab claw, as their ridged surface curved around the arm and ended in spikes that could be used for stabbing. They were held to the body by a handgrip and an arm strap; the latter could be used alone so that the shield hand was free to grip the stone when the Orc was climbing. It can also be seen as an attempt to manufacture in metal their own version of the Balrog's wing.

ARMOR

As mentioned earlier, there is a theory that the Orcs of Moria sought to remake themselves in the image of the Balrog as they perceived it. This can be seen when comparing examples of their armor to the written and illustrated descriptions that exist of the hopefully now-extinct demon spirit.

The helmet (*top*) consisted of two pieces, the skull and the visor, both of which had spikes extending into the face area, and these were riveted together at a point in front of the ears in such a way as to give the impression of a fanged maw. It also served to limit the amount of light shining on their sensitive eyes. The skull had a jagged crest which can be seen to bear a close similarity to the Balrog's flaming mane.

Some Moria Orcs appear to have worn mail hauberks under their other armor, whereas most seem to have scavenged cloth from the Dwarves; it is unlikely that the red-dyed fabric would have been produced in Moria by Orcish hands. All examples that have been recovered were threadbare, little more than rags, but the telltale signs of Dwarven design can still be faintly detected. Over these garments was worn a very basic and crude collar, cuirass (*right*), fauld and set of pauldrons, each consisting of no more than three or four metal plates that had been riveted together; again, these were fashioned into sections that resembled a carapace or scales, the jagged edges and pointed tips being suggestive of flames. The Orcs also wore leather gauntlets (*below right*), which had the curious embellishment of pointed fingertips: it is easy to see these as being designed to give additional grip when climbing, but they are also reminiscent of claws. Although not commonplace, some examples of crude shoes have been found, consisting of little more than a sole to protect the foot from sharp stones and other debris, which was secured to the foot by means of two leather straps.

Gandalf

Despite all that is recorded in the Red Book and other related tales of the history of Middle-earth, little is actually known about who Gandalf [TA c. 1000 –] was. Elven writings say that he came out of the West at the closing of the tenth century of the Third Age. In appearance he was like an old man, clad in robes and stooped but still hale. Some writers believe that this humble mien was a way to make his advice more palatable to the mighty whom he guided. It is written that of the Five Istari, or wizards, to come to Middle-earth he was the last but, as Círdan perceived immediately, perhaps the greatest. For this reason, Círdan gave to him Narya, his Elven-ring of Fire, for he saw that Gandalf would have need of it in the trials ahead. Sauron had used fire and flame to terrify, torture and destroy; with Narya, Gandalf would kindle the fire in Men's hearts, and provide a beacon in the darkness to which all the Free Peoples could rally.

Gandalf was forbidden by the Powers from challenging Sauron directly, but that did not prevent him from battling the Dark Lord's servants and allies. He used Glamdring on many occasions: killing Orcs in both Moria and Mordor; dispatching Saruman's Uruk-hai and, most significantly, slaying the Balrog. This heroic feat could not have been achieved by any of the Fellowship save him, for Balrogs were of the Maiar, and as such could be killed only by one of equal rank who possessed a similarly noble weapon. Without Gandalf, the Fellowship, along with the hopes of the Free Peoples, would have died in the black pit of Moria. Such was the terrible might and power of the Balrog that Gandalf

ABOVE *Gandalf was given Narya, the Ring of Fire, by Círdan of the Grey Havens.*
RIGHT *Gandalf wielded Glamdring at the Black Gate against Sauron's army.*

the Grey also died atop Zirak-zigil, his part in the Quest of Mount Doom seemingly at an end; but the Powers sent him back, renewed and invigorated, as Gandalf the White. From this point, no mortal weapon could harm him and his powers were such that he was able to overpower Saruman, Chief of the Order of Istari, leaving him to his ruin at the hands of a lowly wretch.

Despite Gandalf's achievements with a sword, it was his wisdom and knowledge that proved most useful in the War of the Ring. Like the other Istari, Gandalf was sent to Middle-earth to counsel and to aid with knowledge. During the two thousand years of his time among the peoples of Middle-earth he traveled constantly, moving from the north kingdom of Arnor to the desert tribes of Harad in the south, trying to rouse them to challenge the Dark Lord's might and advise on the best way to defend their realms. The welcome he received varied greatly: the Elves loved and respected him, embracing the wizard as one of their own; the rulers of Men in Gondor and Rohan were more ambivalent, recognizing in Gandalf's schemes and power plays that they were being used as pawns in a larger game; among the Haradrim he encountered fear and even open hostility. In Elrond and Aragorn he found two allies who would prove critical in helping him succeed in his great task, and in the hobbits Frodo and Sam, two indefatigable bearers of the Ring to its destruction, but it was Gandalf who devised the strategy by which Sauron was finally overthrown, distracting the enemy at Helm's Deep and at Gondor and then with one final desperate gamble outside the Black Gate of Mordor itself, each feint a bold act of prestidigitation worthy of the greatest of magicians.

The Red Book states that the light in his eyes danced with the spirit of one who was greater than those he walked among; perhaps he truly was one of the Maiar, the immortal spirits who served the Valar in the Undying Lands in the Far West. Gandalf never revealed the truth in all this, and when he sailed west with the Last Keepers of the Rings, all that Middle-earth was left with was tales of his great deeds in protecting the lands and people that he loved.

GLAMDRING

Glamdring (a Sindarin word meaning "foe-hammer") was a long, two-handed sword that belonged to King Turgon of the Noldorin Elves. As befitting the exalted status of the high king, Glamdring was of unsurpassed workmanship, and represented the very pinnacle of Elven weaponcraft. After the fall of Gondolin, the sword disappeared, turning up thousands of years later in a troll hoard, where it was claimed by Gandalf. It can only be guessed as to whether he foresaw that the time for war was near at hand. This was the same hoard that yielded Bilbo's – later to be Frodo's – sword, Sting.

Like many Elven blades, Glamdring had a subtle, elongated leaf shape; the cross guard bore a small, uncut, pale blue stone, and is inscribed with runes in Sindarin, which read:

68

Turgon aran Gondolin tortha, Gar a matha J vegil Glamdring
Gûd Daedheloth, Dam an Glamhoth

Turgon king of Gondolin wields, Has and holds the sword Glamdring,
Foe of Morgoth's realm, hammer to the Orcs

This was a strengthening spell to protect the user's hand should an actual blow strike it. The handgrip was fashioned from a piece of wood which was placed over the metal tang, covering about half of it; on this was placed brass wire curled into rings and over these was wrapped a rectangle of wet leather that had been dyed blue in the Elven style, which was tunnel-stitched into a cylindrical sheath to hold all in place. The pommel of Glamdring was unusually large, but this was to keep the long sword perfectly balanced.

Although Glamdring was a two-handed sword, it was so beautifully made and elegant that Gandalf was able to wield it one-handed. The rune inscriptions gave it an added level of power which was crucial in allowing him to slay the Balrog atop Zirak-zigil. Gandalf carried Glamdring with him throughout the War of the Ring, except when he visited Saruman at Orthanc, where perhaps some foresight made him leave it behind, fortuitously storing it in Rivendell. But after the defeat of Sauron and the crowning of King Elessar he laid it aside, along with the burden of his labors, before sailing into the West. It is believed that the sword was for a time an heirloom of the Mirkwood Elves, but later it passed into the safekeeping of King Elessar and is now stored in the treasure vault at Minas Tirith.

The Balrog

A CREATURE OF THE ANCIENT WORLD, and probably the last of its kind, the Balrog of Morgoth fled to the deeps of the bottommost caverns of Khazad-dûm following the destruction of Thangorodrim in the First Age, it is thought, and there became entombed during the reshaping of the world. And there it would have remained if not for the avarice and industry of the Dwarves of Moria, who were following the rich vein of mithril ever deeper into the earth. So it was that some two thousand years into the Third Age they released this demon, and doom came upon them: the Balrog slew many Dwarves, including their king, Durin VI, and those who escaped its onslaught fled their kingdom forever. For the next thousand years, Khazad-dûm had only one lord and master, but gradually it gained a vast host of subjects, as Orcs descended out of the Misty Mountains to populate the vacant kingdom. To them, the Balrog must have been akin to a god, to be venerated and feared in equal measure, but it must be supposed that even the Balrog was, to some degree, acting under the control of Sauron, who would have been aware of the Balrog even from afar. News would also have come to the White Council of what the Dwarves had unleashed, so Gandalf was well aware of what he might face should the Fellowship travel through the dark halls of Khazad-dûm.

The Red Book of Westmarch records that in appearance the Balrog was "a creature of shadow and flame" that had both a whip and a sword of fire; earlier accounts, taken from the library at Rivendell, mention that the Balrogs of Morgoth would sometimes take to the battlefield bearing a great black axe or mace, although the whip remained its primary choice. It seems very likely

TOP RIGHT *Artist's impression of the creature of "shadow and flame."*
RIGHT *The Balrog pursued the Fellowship through Moria, but perhaps was directed by Sauron.*

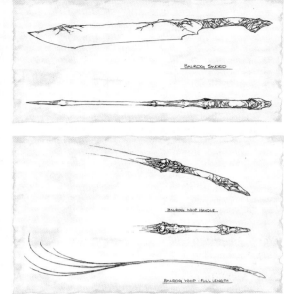

ABOVE *The Balrog was able to draw its weapons from within the core of itself.*
RIGHT *Designs of the sword and whip used by the Balrog in Moria.*

that, being a Maia spirit, the Balrog was able to summon the weapon at will from within the core of itself, be that fire or darkness. There is no doubt that regardless of the weapon, the damage inflicted was terrible indeed, given the combination of size, might and sorcery that went into its use. The Balrog stood some three or four times the height of a man, and had a tail that extended back the same distance again; Frodo wrote that the shadow was "like two vast wings" and that these reached across the width of the hall, a distance that has been estimated to be at least fifty feet.

The Red Book also records that the Balrog appeared to be a match in magical power for Gandalf, who was unable to best it through the use of spellcraft and had to resort to more direct means for dispatching the demon. Since they were both of the Maiar, it is clear that none but Gandalf could have battled the Balrog and won, for no normal weapon could harm them, and even in the glory days of the Elves only the most powerful of the Eldar were able to kill these most dreadful of Morgoth's servants. After an epic ten-day battle that took the two combatants down to the very roots of the mountain and up the Endless Stair to Durin's Tower, here, atop Zirak-zigil, Gandalf finally slew the Balrog.

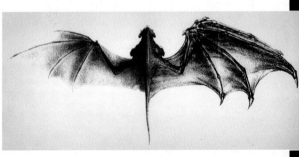

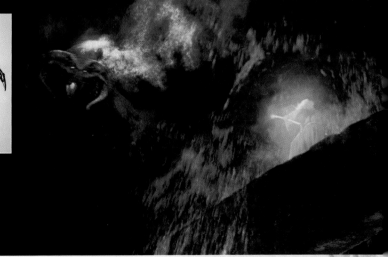

ABOVE *An anatomical study of the winged demon, drawn from the accounts found in the Red Book.*
RIGHT *Gandalf and the Balrog were both Maiar, and were a match in magical power.*

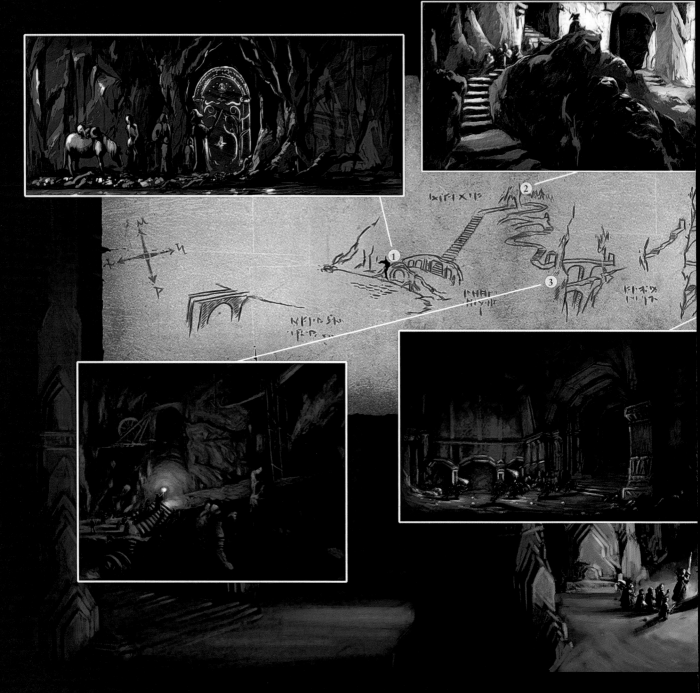

The Mines of Moria plan

1. **The West-gate of Moria**
   Also known as the Doors of Durin, they were impenetrable unless one knew the answer to the spell laid on them by Celebrimbor of the Noldorin Elves of Eregion.

2. **New mine workings**
   The Dwarves had delved further and deeper since Gandalf last visited them; even the wise Wizard was confounded for a time.

3. **The Mithril Mines**
   The Dwarves' greed and pursuit of the priceless treasure led them deep down, into the very heart of Caradhras. The mine workings were located along narrow ledges in sheer-sided chasms.

4. **The Great Hall of the Dwarrowdelf**
   This was the greatest chamber in the entire kingdom of Moria, or Khazad-dûm as it was in the Dwarvish language of Khuzdul. All lay in darkness at the time of the War of the Ring.

5. **The Chamber of Mazarbul**
   This chamber was located off to the side of the Great Hall of the Dwarrowdelf. Here was found Balin's

Tomb, and the Book of Mazarbul, or Book of Records, which recounts the rise and fall of Balin's folk, the last Dwarves ever to live in Moria. The walls apparently carried an additional record of the Dwarves' time there.

6. **The Stairs of Khazad-dûm**

Located at the end of the Great Hall, these stairs led down to the lower levels, and a smaller chamber through which was found the Bridge.

7. **The Bridge of Khazad-dûm**

The narrow bridge provided excellent security at the eastern edge of the kingdom, for it would only allow for visitors to come over in single file. Should the enemy overpower the Dwarf guards at the East-gate they would be picked off by the Dwarves who manned each end of the bridge. It was never rebuilt following the battle between Gandalf and the Balrog.

8. **The East-gate**

This gate led out to the Vale of Anduin, and from here the Elven realm of Lothlórien could be reached, although none before the Fellowship dared to do – Gimli was the first Dwarf to set foot in the domain of the Lady Galadriel. The steep ground outside the East-gate was the site of the last great battle in the war between the Dwarves and the Orcs, in which the Dwarves were victorious.

Amon Hen

Amon Hen was a watchtower and outpost established at the northern frontier of the kingdom of Gondor during the Second Age. At the time of the War of the Ring it too, like Amon Sûl, had long been abandoned and fallen into ruin. The last remaining feature of this once-extensive building was the Seeing Seat, an observation point situated at the top of the hill and overlooking the River Anduin, which lay far below. From here, the captain of the garrison would have had an uninterrupted view of all the terrain north, south and east of its position. It is likely that a beacon was always maintained, ready to light in case there was a need to warn Gondor of approaching attack.

The Fellowship made camp by the shore of Nen Hithoel; it was a good defensive position, offering escape back into their boats if they were attacked from the woods, and solid cover from the trees that bordered the lake.

As is known from Frodo's account in the Red Book, he was approached by Boromir and was urged by him to go to Gondor so the Ring could be used against the Enemy. Frodo resisted and Boromir became angry and desperate; Frodo's fear at what Boromir might do led him to put on the Ring and flee, ending up at the Seeing Seat. In the meantime, Aragorn and the rest of the group had begun to search for them in the woods that covered the hill. At

ABOVE *Eagles formed the Seeing Seat; probably used because of their keen eyesight.*
RIGHT *Architectural conceptual study of Amon Hen in the Second Age.*
BOTTOM *The Seeing Seat as seen from the east bank of the Anduin.*

One hundred Uruk-hai converged on the Seeing Seat.

this time an Uruk-hai raiding party entered the woods from the western side.

Frodo and Aragorn confronted each other at the top of the hill, and it was at this point that Frodo made his choice to break the Fellowship. Frodo now truly understood how evil the Ring was, and knew that sooner or later it would corrupt all his friends. In making that decision to walk alone into the land of the Dark Lord, Frodo showed that the hobbits, the little people, were possessed of the greatest courage. One hundred Uruk-hai were drawn to the Seeing Seat and Frodo, so in order to give him as much time to escape as possible, Aragorn stepped forward to face them. Aragorn did not carry a shield or wear heavy armor, so any blow would seriously disable or even kill him. Instead, he relied on his speed, reflexes and ability with a sword, skills he had learned from the Elves. The Uruks were armored and had a brutal strength, but they moved and attacked with a lumbering predictability that allowed the heavily outnumbered Ranger to kill many without taking serious injury to himself.

When Legolas and Gimli joined the fray, there was a short but intense period of close combat. This suited Aragorn and Gimli, who had hand weapons, but Legolas had to use his two white knives as much as his bow. Nevertheless, such was the dazzling speed of

Dozens of Uruk warriors were slain by the Fellowship.

the Elf that he was able to nock and fire his arrows at Uruks who were close enough to strike him before they had time to complete their swing.

Then Boromir sounded the horn of Gondor – a distress call that would have been heard for miles – which prompted his friends to begin forging a path through the Uruks to him. The Uruks were also heading toward him, so there was literally a running battle between the two sides. As Legolas and Gimli battled dozens of remaining Uruks, Aragorn raced on to help his comrade. But when he reached Boromir the damage had already been done: Boromir lay dying, with three black arrows in his body. Yet before Aragorn could go to him he was faced with the leader of the raiding party. Although battle-fatigued, Aragorn fought hand-to-hand with the creature, needing all his skills to finally best it. And so Boromir of Gondor was avenged. The victory for the Fellowship was not complete, however, for some of the raiding party escaped, taking with them the two hobbits Merry and Pippin. Aragorn knew that Frodo had made his choice, and so decided to lead the remnant of the Fellowship in pursuit of the hobbits, into the kingdom of Rohan.

Rohan

THE KINGDOM OF ROHAN was originally called Calenardhon, and was merely a northern province of Gondor. Although its wide grassy plains were sparsely populated by the Dúnedain, they did build two great structures to defend its western border: the impregnable fortress of Angrenost, or Isengard as it was known in Rohan, and the mighty refuge of Helm's Deep. Each sat but a few leagues north and south of the Gap of Rohan and the Fords of Isen. Calenardhon's other borders were the River Limlight in the north, which flowed out of Fangorn Forest, the White Mountains in the south, and in the east the wide marshy area known as the Mouths of Entwash, which flowed into the River Anduin just south of the Emyn Muil.

The long wars of the Third Age had further reduced the population of Calenardhon, so when, in TA 2510, a great host of Orcs and Easterlings crossed the River Anduin and invaded from the north, Gondor had to send its army a great distance. Out of position and fatigued, it suffered heavy losses and would have been defeated but for the unlooked-for arrival of Men from the north led by Eorl. These Northmen were well mounted and equipped as heavy cavalry, and their onslaught was too great for the enemy to withstand. All of the Orcs and Easterlings who were not cut down on the marshy ground fled east back across the river. The Northmen's epic 600-mile journey south through Wilderland along the length of the Anduin is one of the great rides of any age. In gratitude for this heroic deed, and surely not without a little self-interest, Cirion, the Ruling Steward of Gondor, granted Eorl all of the lands of Calenardhon.

When Eorl led his people into their new home, he named it the Riddermark, land of the horse-lords; ever after in Gondor it was known as Rohan, "land of horses," for Eorl's people were famed for their skill with their special breed of horses, the mearas. Rohan was a green and fertile land, ideally suited to the rearing of horses, and their masters raised great herds which were renowned throughout Middle-earth. The people of Rohan

Elven map of Rohan recovered from Helm's Deep, perhaps carried by Haldir.

lived in small settlements, some farming the land and some following the herds across the wide plains as they moved from pasture to pasture. Few of the Rohan lived in the east, as this low-lying land was marshy and therefore unsuited to both man and horse.

The large open spaces of Rohan made it difficult to defend, but they also made it difficult to overcome, as its population was scattered throughout the land. However, both Rohan and Gondor benefited greatly from their alliance, each coming to the other's aid in times of need. Although Rohan was left to stand alone against the sudden and traitorous attack from the west, an older alliance helped it prevail, and allowed Rohan to ride to Gondor in its greatest hour of need.

EDORAS

Edoras was the capital of the kingdom of Rohan, built by Eorl and Brego, the first and second kings of Rohan, during the twenty-sixth century of the Third Age, and the place where its kings ruled. As the capital, it had a much

---

RIGHT *The famed stables at Edoras.*
BELOW *The city of Edoras commanded views of the White Mountains.*

larger population than any other settlement in Rohan – it is estimated that there were at least two hundred separate dwellings at the end of the Third Age – and this made Edoras unique in that its people consumed more food than they produced. They were dependent on the produce of nearby settlements, so trade was brisk, creating much traffic throughout the region. The road that led to the great outer gate passed through two lines of barrows: on the west were nine tombs of kings of the first line, from Eorl through to Helm; on the east were those of the second line, from Fréalof through to Thengel and Théoden's son, Théodred, killed by Saruman's Orcs. This served as a potent reminder to all visitors of how highly the people of Rohan honored their kings. Edoras was also home to a magnificent stable, in which Shadowfax had a large area set aside just for him. There were also fewer farmers in Edoras, as many of the men served in the Royal Guard. If they were not on duty

The Golden Hall of Meduseld was the Courts of the King.

at Meduseld, the Golden Hall and Royal Seat of the king, they were away at other settlements on royal business. In fact, the duties of a great many of the people of Edoras were directly bound up in the daily life of the king and his household. With so many doubly beholden to the king, Wormtongue, who acted in the king's name, effectively dominated the entire population as well as their monarch.

Although the position of Edoras made it ideally suited to defending, as it was located on an isolated, steep-sided foothill close to the Ered Nimrais, the White Mountains, and water was readily available from the Snow-bourn, which flowed nearby, it was not a true stronghold. In times of trouble, the people of Edoras would have fled to the Hold of Dunharrow, which was a few miles upstream. In the five hundred years since Edoras has been built, its palisade walls had already been breached, in the winter of TA 2758 during a great Dunlending invasion, so King Théoden was all too aware that Edoras could not protect his people for long. He was unfortunate to live in changing times, and he became the first king in Rohan's history to abandon Edoras voluntarily in search of safety when tribes of Wild Men out of Dunland, who had been incited by Saruman, overran the outlying settlements of Rohan and began heading toward its capital. Fortunately for the people of Edoras, who emerged after the Battle of Helm's Deep, the rabble never made it to their capital: a combination of disorganization and encounters with the Rohirrim had dispersed them, and those that survived evidently withdrew to Dunland.

DUNHARROW

When the Northmen began exploring their new land, the most ancient and mysterious site they found was the Hold of Dunharrow, a fortress and refuge built in prehistoric times by Mountain Men. It consisted of a steep, switchback path that rose hundreds of feet to a wide grassy plateau surrounded on all sides by the White Mountains; the path, bordered by standing stones, continued across the plateau and through a dark wooded glen that was the haunted pass of Dimholt, until it reached a

The banners of kings past and present hung behind the throne.

small dark doorway. This was the beginning of the Paths of the Dead.

After their encounter with the White Wizard Saruman at Orthanc Théoden, Gandalf and Aragorn took counsel. In many ways their hand had been forced by Pippin, who had stolen a look into the palantír of Orthanc, which had been recovered from the deposed Saruman. This ill-judged glance had drawn the Dark Lord's Eye to him, as well as to his location in Rohan. Soon the land would be overrun with Sauron's Orcs as he sought to claim back his Ring. In order to further misdirect the enemy, and also buy Théoden's Rohirrim some time, Gandalf took Pippin and rode with great speed on Shadowfax, Lord of Horses, to Minas Tirith. King Théoden led his Rohirrim, together with Aragorn, Legolas and Gimli, to Dunharrow. At this stage, it had become clear to Théoden that Saruman's attack on Helm's Deep was just the first strike in a wider war, and soon Sauron would launch his own far greater assault upon Gondor and thence across the rest of Middle-earth. As he rode east across Rohan, he sent riders out to call all men to arms, to join him at Dunharrow. The plateau of Dunharrow soon became filled with a sea of tents as the company of the Rohirrim gathered.

At this time Elrond arrived alone at Théoden's tent with a mighty gift for Aragorn. He had brought with him the shards of Narsil, now reforged by the smiths of Rivendell as Andúril, "Flame of the West." No doubt the return of this potent symbol of Aragorn's heritage strengthened his resolve to challenge Sauron's might and enabled him to take his fateful journey through the Paths of the Dead. As Aragorn, Legolas and Gimli began their journey into the dark, the chain of beacon fires begun in Minas Tirith reached the Men of Rohan. War had begun in Gondor, and despite having only six thousand spears instead of the hoped-for ten, Théoden led his Rohirrim on a famous charge. The distance from Dunharrow to Minas Tirith was 102 leagues, or 306 miles, and the Rohirrim covered this in just three days, arriving in time to break the Siege of Gondor and instigate the Battle of the Pelennor Fields.

Théoden mustered six thousand spears to the encampment at Dunharrow.

79

Wild Men of Dunland

IN THE YEARS OF THE SECOND AGE before the Númenóreans settled in Middle-earth, primitive hillmen inhabited the lands west and south of the Misty Mountains, as far down as the valleys surrounding the White Mountains. Uncultured and superstitious, they were wary of the tall men who came out of the west, and came to fear and hate them. They were hunted and persecuted in such numbers that they had dwindled by the start of the Third Age. At this time they had come to congregate in the valleys of the White Mountains and the grassy plains of Dunland, which lay west of the Misty Mountains between Moria and Isengard; a few went north, and became the ancestors of the Men of Bree. Dunland then became the area most populated by these men, who came to be called Dunlendings.

When Eorl and his people were granted Calenardhon – Rohan, as it would later be known – in TA 2510, they drove the Wild Men from their new lands, earning their bitter hatred and enmity. The Wild Men were also driven from the Ered Nimrais by the Men of Gondor. During the next five hundred years these swarthy, dark-haired savages made frequent attacks upon the outlying settlements of Rohan, exacting revenge upon the usurpers, whom they called "straw-heads" because of the high number of blond warriors among them. As a consequence, Rohan maintained patrols and garrisons to the west at the Fords of Isen to try to limit the number of raids, although these patrols had virtually disappeared under Wormtongue's stewardship, to the point where Saruman's forces could make incursions almost at will.

Yet not everybody took against the Wild Men. At some point near the end of the thirtieth century of the Third Age Saruman made contact with them, and swayed them to his side by playing on their resentment and hatred of those who had taken what was theirs. Saruman welcomed to Orthanc a large warband of these Dunlendings, led by a tribal chief named Wulf. Saruman evidently convinced them that they could reclaim what had been taken, and during the early part of TA 3019 a fearsome raiding force comprising Dunlendings, Orcs and Uruk-hai left Isengard and began ravaging the western settlements of Rohan. Previous attacks by Orcs and Uruk-hai

The Wild Men were armed by Saruman's Orcs before striking out into the Westfold.

Saruman incited the Wild Men by reminding them of the wrongs done to them.

had killed many Rohirrim at the Fords of Isen, so there were no warriors to defend against this surprise attack. Many people of Rohan were killed in these attacks, but the raiders never made it across the country to Edoras; it is fair to assume that they encountered one or more *éoreds*, companies of mounted warriors, who would have been patrolling the interior, perhaps even the many thousands of Rohirrim led by Éomer and Gandalf who were riding hard to Helm's Deep. In any event, this would be the last time that the Wild Men made a concerted attack upon the people of Rohan.

The Wild Men, or Dunlendings, were hill-folk, used to living in harsh conditions with little to protect them from the elements. As a result they were tough, hardy people, big and powerful, with long, unkempt hair and beards. Their primitive level of technology meant that their weapons were crude, all derived from a club. Any weapon that had an element of metal to it would have been taken from a Rohan settlement or given to them by Saruman. There appears to have been no weapon of choice. The Wild Men had no sophisticated fighting style, but instead relied upon their strength to beat someone to death with a clubbing action, using whatever weapon came to hand. If a staff weapon was carried, it would probably have been a farming implement such as a pitchfork or hoe, or a crude kind of halberd forged by the Orc blacksmiths in Isengard. Wild Men did not wear armor; their only clothing was the skins and furs that they had cut from the carcasses of hunted beasts. As the men of Middle-earth

prospered and became sophisticated, their primitive cousins dwindled, receding into the shadows until they became little more than a memory, a fireside tale to delight and terrify adults and children alike.

TOP RIGHT *The Wild Men's leader, Wulf, swore a blood oath to Saruman.*
RIGHT *They harrowed the land of Rohan, burning the villages and killing everyone in their path.*

Wargs & Warg-riders

WARGS

WARG WAS THE NAME THAT MEN GAVE to the giant wolves that roamed Rhovanion – also known as Wilderland – and the wilds to the west of the Misty Mountains. However, the name originally applied to the terrifying werewolves that plagued Middle-earth: these evil spirits took form only at night, preying on the flesh of anything that they caught. Fortunately, by the Third Age they had apparently all but disappeared. Like so many foul creatures, the Warg may have first been bred in Mordor, the result of mixing two beasts to produce a true monster.

Far from being dumb beasts, the Wargs of the Third Age were intelligent predators; it is believed that they had a crude understanding of some Orc words and may even have possessed their own language. Wargs hunted in packs, surrounding their prey and closing in or making feints to distract the prey's attention so that it could be attacked on its blind side. Frodo records in the Red Book that Wargs harried the Fellowship on their journey south before entering Moria.

From skeletons found in Rohan, we know that Wargs measured between five and six feet at the shoulder, and could be up to fifteen feet in length from snout to tail; cautious estimates put the weight of these monsters at a minimum of 400 pounds, around three times that of a man. Rohan tapestries show the Wargs to have a bearlike face with a long muzzle full of huge fangs and a long, prehensile neck; its eyes were small and set back to each side of its snout, and its ears were at the back of the skull. This arrangement gave the greatest sensory range while keeping its vulnerable areas protected, and the long neck gave it reach, flexibility and power when biting into flesh, whether the belly or neck of a horse, or through a warrior's armor. There was a large bulge above its forelegs, which contained massive muscles that propelled it at speed and allowed the Warg to tear its prey apart. Apart from its ruff, the Warg had short dense fur, which would have kept injuries from tooth and claw to a minimum. Not all harm would have come from the men and beasts that it was attacking: Wargs were

Wargs were tireless hunters that could outrun a horse over a short distance.

Powerful haunches and a thumb on the front paw allowed the Warg to climb.

known to be ferocious and could quickly turn on other members of their pack as well as their handlers. Coloration and patterning of the fur seemed to vary throughout the breed, with stripes, mottling and other patterns appearing in shades of tan, ginger, liver, white and brown, with harder patterning appearing toward the back of the creature. Despite their size, Wargs could move very quickly: they could run at a measured pace over long stretches and in short bursts could overtake a horse. When attacking, a Warg would generate as much speed as possible and throw itself at its prey; while its thick skull and powerful forequarters would absorb the blow, the prey would be stunned into immobility, allowing the Warg to tear into it at its leisure.

Wargs were unusual among the predators of Middle-earth in that they formed an alliance of sorts with Orcs of the Misty Mountains. It is not known how or when this happened, or indeed why; an alliance is a mutually beneficial thing, and where it can be seen that a mounted Warg would give the Orcs their own cavalry, able to make fast and devastating raids upon their enemy, there can have been little additional benefit for the Wargs. It may be that the Wargs were partially "tamed" by the Orcs' offering them meat from their kills over a period of time, until the Wargs became used to their scent. Then there would have been a prolonged period of establishing contact, which would no doubt have been fraught with peril: many Orcs would have ended up inside their allies rather than on top of them. Nevertheless, it is evident that they succeeded in getting the Wargs to accept being mounted and ridden, and in so doing became a deadly menace to the other races of Middle-earth.

Sauron used Wargs at the Siege of Gondor. The great beasts carried Orc captains, who rode alongside the massed ranks of Sauron's Orcish army. Because of the great size of the force marching upon Minas Tirith, it would have otherwise been impossible to maintain effective communication with the Orc soldiers or between battalions so that they acted in concert – something Sauron may have learned from his defeat at the hands of the Last Alliance three thousand years before. The Orc captains used the Wargs to ride up and down the ranks, shouting commands; just before the start of assault by catapult, one surviving sergeant-at-arms noted in his journal that Wargs were seen charging along the front lines where the catapults had been situated, their riders carrying a burning brand, evidently as a signal to begin the bombardment. Despite their appearance at the siege, there was no separate division of Warg cavalry; this may be because of their unpredictable nature, because an insufficient number were available to Mordor to put together a division, or perhaps because Sauron did not anticipate facing a mounted defense from the largely infantry-based Men of Gondor. The arrival of the Men of Rohan, brought about by the failure of Saruman's army of Uruk-hai, was just one of many crucial oversights made by the enemy – oversights that ultimately led to his downfall.

WARG-RIDERS

The Orcs who eventually became Warg-riders were smaller and lighter than others of their kind, and could evidently bear to suffer daylight more than ordinary Orcs. Many carried horrific scarring and other injuries, including missing hands, caused by not giving their ferocious and carnivorous allies enough respect. They managed to ride the Wargs by means of a crude saddle made of hide that was strapped around the beast and sat just behind its hump. Their preferred method of attack was to let the Warg do all the initial work, and if there was any dispatching to be done, they would dismount, if it was safe to do so, and finish off the hapless victim. When riding into battle against Men of Rohan, the Orcs would slash at their enemy from the backs of their mounts, using crude scimitars and knives. Often the agile creatures would lean down at the last moment, avoiding the spears of their foe, and slice at the bellies of the horses; once the warrior had tumbled to the ground, Warg and rider would compete to finish him off.

A small leather saddle prevented the rider from falling off the Warg.

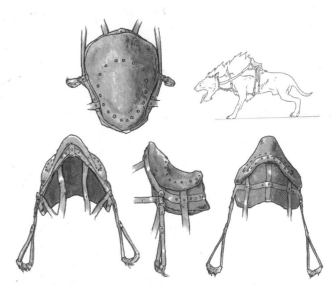

WEAPONS

Despite their being mounted, there is no real evidence to suggest that the Warg-riders favored either bows or spears, even though these would have been highly effective weapons to use. It may be that the bucking motion of the Warg made it almost impossible to aim either weapon with any accuracy. Although the occasional bow or pike has been found, it appears that they generally carried crude, single-edged scimitars and sometimes also knives, which were used to slash at their enemy as they passed them. The scimitars were about two and a half feet long and lacked either guard or pommel; the handgrip was just a strip of leather wrapped around the tang. The knives bore some similarity to the Moria Orc swords; evidently this design of extending the cutting edge to the pommel was one that was much favored among Orc-kind.

84

ARMOR

Their armor was unique to the Warg-riders, and unique within this group: some, such as their leader (allegedly named Sharkû, perhaps in reference to his great age), wore little beyond bone and fur, whereas others preferred to be more heavily protected, wearing multiple layers of rotting hide, fur and hair or mail, but nearly all included something from the remains of the Warg's kill, such as bone and tooth, and from parts of the Warg itself. Keeping their weight down was a factor with most in order not to tire the Warg. Sharkû's relative lack of protection may have been a status symbol: as the leader and longest-surviving member of the pack, he may have been demonstrating to the others that he needed no barrier between himself and the monsters they shared their lives with.

Their cuirass was often made from the bones of a horse's rib cage, to which was stitched pieces of hide and fur; during centuries of wear – if the Orc survived his close contact with the Wargs, living with and feeding them as they did – the Warg-rider's armor would go from foul-smelling to rotten, and so would need to be constantly repaired and replaced. Fresh hide would be stitched on top of old, and bones would be replaced as they disintegrated. Other parts of the Orc's body would be wrapped in hide that had been reinforced with bone, and adorned with Warg fangs and spikes made from sharpened bone, to protect it from both enemy and ally. The armor may have been further strengthened by bonding pieces together with glue made by boiling down horse bones and hooves. Some Orcs wore helmets made from the skulls and scalps of their kills, both beasts and men, and these often featured grisly crests of bone. A rough cloak of Warg fur would have completed the outfit. Almost as important as protecting the Orc, this armor would have exuded familiar scents to the Warg, especially from the fur, and in this way served to further insinuate the idea that the Orc was part of the Warg's pack. The Orc carried no shield, as both hands would be needed to hold on to the sword and the Warg.

85

The Defense of Helm's Deep

S AURON THE DARK LORD had commanded Saruman to build him an army that could be used to overrun the Men of Rohan. Although some of the Orcs of the Misty Mountains had been drawn into the White Wizard's service, they had probably been dismissed by him as an effective fighting force because they were weakened in daylight. Any Orcish army crossing the wide plains of Rohan would have been an easy target for the mounted Rohirrim while they rested during the day, whereas the Uruk-hai would march until they died. They had already begun to make forays with the Wild Men into Rohan, and these raids had prompted King Théoden to decide to withdraw his people to a safe haven. Instead of leading them to the Hold of Dunharrow, which was just a few miles away up into the Ered Nimrais, Théoden made the decision to go west to Helm's Deep, an ancient stone refuge wedged into a narrow steep-sided valley.

Helm's Deep is said to have been built during the early days of Gondor by the Dúnedain with the aid of giants; whether true or not, its thick stone walls had never been breached, so Théoden would have felt justifiably confident that his people would be safe there. In TA 2758, when Rohan was overrun by Easterlings and Dunlendings, Helm Hammerhand had led his people to this refuge and stayed there throughout the siege and long winter that followed. Such were his deeds during this time that he became one of Rohan's most famous

RIGHT *The Uruk-hai had been trained to fight in disciplined, ordered ranks.*
BELOW *Helm's Deep was wedged into a narrow rocky valley; it was said to have been built by giants.*

Ten thousand Uruk-hai presented themselves to their lord and master, Saruman.

kings, and the refuge was named in his honor. Helm's Deep consisted of the Hornburg, a 300-foot-high tower that was surrounded by circular inner and outer ramparted walls, the outer standing 100 feet above the ground; the only entrance was the Great Gates, huge wooden doors set between two guard towers, which were approached by a curving stone causeway. Within the inner court were archways that had been carved into the living rock, leading to the halls, quarters, stables and armory. It is likely that a small garrison was maintained here, rotated seasonally, perhaps one of the first duties assigned to young soldiers of Rohan, or to its veterans, in order to keep its memory alive in the minds of the people. They would have ensured that food and water was always replenished and that supplies were not stolen. Connecting the Hornburg with the other side of the ravine was the Deeping Wall, a wall over 30 feet high and nearly 300 feet long. Its rampart was wide enough for four men to stand abreast. The whole structure was solid stone apart from the gates and a small culvert set at the base of the Deeping Wall. Almost impregnable...

With no time to muster his Rohirrim, who ranged far and wide across the plains of Rohan, Théoden must have felt that it was the easier of the two to defend, given the few warriors at his disposal. (When Éomer had been banished by Wormtongue, he had ridden north with all the Rohirrim in Edoras still loyal to the king, leaving Théoden with just his Royal Guard, together with those who could be gathered from the settlements nearby.) If circumstances had been different, those few would never have been enough, regardless of the strength of the stone walls, and Rohan would have been annihilated.

But the tide was beginning to turn: although a new power was rising among the forces of evil, an old alliance was about to be remembered among the Free Peoples, and faith rekindled in their hearts. The Battle of Helm's Deep would be one of the finest hours for Men and Elves in the Third Age.

When Saruman realized that his raiding party of Uruk-hai was not going to return with the halfling Ring-bearer, he had good reason to believe that they had failed and that more direct action was needed. The attempt to seize the Ring was a desperate gamble on his part. Blinded by arrogance and a lust for power, Saruman believed, mistakenly, that with the Ring in his possession he would be Lord of the

The Uruk-hai would have covered the twenty-league distance to Helm's Deep in about a day.

Rings and Middle-earth, and all would submit to him. Having already betrayed the Free Peoples, and now attempting to betray his "ally," Sauron, Saruman found his position becoming dangerously isolated. Perhaps he hoped that by destroying the Men of Rohan, as well as the last of Isildur's line he would gain some bargaining power with the Dark Lord. Whatever the reason, shortly after Wormtongue's arrival at Isengard, armed with the traitorous intelligence that he clearly supplied, Saruman sent his army of ten thousand Uruk-hai to war.

It was about twenty leagues, or 60 miles, from Isengard to Helm's Deep, a distance that would probably have been completed by the tireless Uruk-hai in a day. The siege ladders were carried by teams of sappers safely positioned in the middle of the battalions, but the heavier giant crossbows must have taken longer to arrive; however, this may have been factored into Saruman's strategy, as they were employed only during a later stage of the battle.

Saruman had clearly been preparing this assault for some time. During the centuries that he had occupied Orthanc he had traveled extensively throughout the area and likely had visited Helm's Deep on a number of occasions, learning its structure in detail. Although

Wormtongue probably supplied information about its one weak spot, Saruman would already have thought of this; indeed, he had prepared his bombs specifically to exploit this chink in the refuge's armor. He also knew that his Uruk army would possibly face attack by the Rohirrim as they marched to the stronghold, and so equipped them specifically to defend against this threat. The first line of defense was the crossbow, which could be used to deadly effect against the armor of the mounted warriors. If the Rohirrim evaded these missiles, they would face a massed rank of pikesmen carrying eighteen-foot pikes, which would be braced in the ground ready to skewer the approaching horses and their riders. If any riders got past these, there were countless swordsman behind the pikes, armed with long, single-edged swords that had a cruel spike on the back which could be used to hook a passing cloak or trip or gash the horse. As it happened, there were no Rohirrim in the Westfold, and so the Uruks advanced unmolested and arrived at night still ten thousand strong.

The arrival of two hundred Elves from Lórien greatly boosted the flagging spirits of the Men of Rohan, but many were unsure of what they would face and whether they could mount an effective defense. Théoden was woefully short of fighting men: even by taking every man and boy who could carry a weapon – some as young as seven, some ten times that – the defenders still only numbered about five hundred, and many carried swords and bows that were antiques even in that long-distant time, the blades pitted, dull-edged and rusting, the strings frayed and the staves slack. Yet these Men of Rohan were prepared to fight to defend their wives, mothers and children, to the death, if necessary; it was their only choice. On the battlements, barrels filled with extra arrows were placed at regular intervals for the Elven archers, who waited patiently to meet their foe.

With nightfall came the start of a heavy rainstorm, perhaps summoned by Saruman to aid his Uruk-hai. In the gloom, and above the sound of the rain, the defenders could hear the stamp of approaching feet and perceive torches burning fitfully in the distance, but it was not until lightning flashed, illuminating the whole valley, that the scale of the threat became apparent. A sea of Uruk-hai, stretching from one side of the valley to the other, marched toward them, and kept on coming until they stood just a hundred paces from the wall. For many on the ramparts, this was as close as they had come to an Uruk; the armored, six-foot monster would have been a terrifying sight on its own, but there were

thousands upon thousands of them waiting to attack.

King Théoden commanded his men, who filled the ramparts of the Hornburg, while Aragorn and Haldir led the Elves of Lórien. As the Uruk-hai beat their pikes upon the ground and chanted their battle cry, arrows were nocked along the length of Helm's Deep. Tension grew until, it is alleged, an old warrior by the name of Aldor, who could no longer hold back his bowstring, let fly an arrow straight into the neck of an Uruk, killing it. This unexpected event signaled the start of the battle: arrows were loosed by the Elves on the wall and by the reinforcements who waited in Helm's Gate, and volley after volley was sent down by the Men of Rohan. Hundreds of Uruks fell under this hail, but the fire was returned by Uruk crossbowmen, and many of the defenders were killed as the thick black bolts punched through their armor. For the men, this was a new phenomenon: they were not used to fighting an enemy who had range weapons, let alone ones that had greater power and range than theirs. Already frightened by the sheer number of attackers, the Men of Rohan suffered a serious loss of morale over their enemy's technological advantage. Meanwhile, Legolas and Gimli, who were fighting near each other, began a competition to see who could kill the most Uruk-hai; at the end of a long, bloody night, it was Gimli who emerged victorious, with an unequaled score of 43, just one more than Legolas.

With arrows and bolts hissing back and forth through the rain, Uruk sappers rushed forward carrying siege ladders, and as they were lifted up a Berserker leaped on and was swung toward the rampart; to further help the ladder on its course, a pikesman would use the blade of his pike to grip the rungs and push it up. The Berserkers were the very worst of the

The Uruk-hai halted one hundred paces from the Deeping Wall.

Berserkers leaped onto the ladders as they were raised by Uruk sappers and pikesmen.

Uruk-hai: bigger, stronger and more dangerous, completely without fear and impervious to pain, their sole task was to buy time for the Uruks coming up the ladders behind them. To achieve this they wielded great two-handed swords, scything left and right to cut a swath around the top of the ladder. While the Berserkers were wielding these horrifying weapons, none of the defenders could get near them, and this allowed the Uruks to swarm up the ladders and onto the rampart. The maneuver seriously reduced the damage that the Elves were able to inflict on their foe, as they were forced to drop their bows and draw their swords. With the Elves engaged in this way, the reinforcements waiting in Helm's Gate fired arrows over the wall and into the horde.

Now Saruman's secret weapon was brought forward and used to devastating effect: sappers carried two of his bombs into the culvert, and they were then ignited by a Berserker's torch. The enormous explosion blew up the middle section of the Deeping Wall, sending masses of stone into the air and down upon Elves and Uruk-hai and killing scores of both. The massive shockwave it sent through the defenders was psychological as well as physical, and as they were trying to recover, the Uruks swarmed through the breach. Aragorn led the remaining Elves in a charge against them, and they fought bravely to try to stem the invading horde, but numbers were against them and they were hard pressed to hold their position.

RIGHT *Sappers carried two enormous bombs into the culvert.*
BELOW *Suicide Berserkers ignited them to devastating effect.*

Defenders above the Great Gate bombarded the attackers below who were breaking through with a battering ram.

At this time the Uruks launched an assault upon the Great Gates: they formed a phalanx, a tight group protected by a shell of interlocking shields, and marched up the causeway. Even as Aragorn directed some of the Elven archers to fire upon their flank, many Uruks were pushed off the sides as sappers carried a large battering ram through their midst and began pounding on the gates. Rohan defenders furiously rained down rocks and arrows upon their foe, but the Uruks' armor kept them from harm. The rotting wood of the gates was no match for the iron of Isengard, and soon they had forced their way through. So began a des-

perate attempt to hold the gate: men fired arrows through the breach as Uruk crossbow bolts thudded into them, with wave after wave of Uruks storming up ready to take their place.

Théoden realized that his allies were in danger of being overrun and ordered Aragorn to lead the Elves back to the Keep. Once inside, Aragorn and Gimli went to the aid of Théoden's men by keeping the Uruks back long enough for them to shore up the shattered gates.

But Saruman had another play to make: sappers brought forward huge ballistas, which needed whole teams of Uruks to pull them, load them, winch back the thick cords and hammer down the firing mechanisms to launch giant grappling hooks over the high outer walls of the Hornburg. Once they were in place, dozens of Uruks hauled giant ladders loaded with swordsmen up to the ramparts,

Commanders directed the crews of the ballistas to fire giant grappling hooks over the Hornburg parapets.

91

Using grappling hooks and winches, the Uruks raised giant siege ladders against the Hornburg.

where they quickly began to overwhelm the Men of Rohan. This two-pronged attack left Théoden with no choice but to withdraw his remaining men into the inner keep.

Through all of this he had been forced to react to the moves of Saruman's army, but as the first light of dawn began to creep over the clifftops, he mounted an attack of his own. With the great horn of Helm Hammerhand sounding through the valley, King Théoden, accompanied by Aragorn, led the remainder of his Rohirrim on a noble but doomed ride: as they charged through the marauding Uruks and down the causeway, they came face to face with the thousands more that still filled the valley.

As Théoden and Aragorn led their riders on a last sortie [inset] Éomer and Gandalf arrived and charged into the Uruk flank.

All looked lost, but Gandalf and Éomer finally arrived with two thousand Rohirrim reinforcements, and they charged down a precipitous shale slope into the flank of the Uruk army. This unanticipated counterattack completely wrong-footed the Uruk-hai, as they believed that all their enemy lay within the refuge. As the mounted warriors swept through them, the Uruk-hai were cut down in droves, with spear, axe and sword, and the armored monsters that knew neither fear nor pain, that never retreated, turned from the horse-lords and fled the battlefield. This could have proved disastrous for the men, as the Uruks had a chance to regroup and reform, ready to attack once more, but unknown to all, the Huorns of Fangorn had moved south in the night to block the valley entrance. As the thousands of Uruk-hai fled down the valley they entered the newly arrived forest; legend tells that none of Saruman's army escaped alive, and when the Huorns eventually moved north, not a single trace of them was left.

Forging Swords

IN THE BEGINNING a sword existed only as potential within the bones of the earth and in the mind of its maker, the blacksmith. But before he could begin to put form to his thought he needed the raw material to create it. This came from the mountains of Middle-earth. Wherever there was igneous rock, rock formed through dramatic volcanic pressure, there would be seams of iron, and this iron-rich rock contained the origins of all metal weaponry and armor in Middle-earth.

The Dwarves were the first race to unlock the secrets of the earth, and they delved long and deep to bring them to the surface. Gold and silver were their toys, and mithril was their wealth, but iron was their foundation. Using skills learned from their creator, Aulë the Vala, they fashioned some of the most wondrous weapons ever seen in Middle-earth, including Elendil's sword, Narsil. Yet it is believed that Men learned the secret of mining not from the Dwarves, for they were ever secretive, but from the Númenóreans who voyaged to Middle-earth during the Second Age, teaching the primitive Mannish cultures much that they themselves had learned from the Elves, who were near the equal of the Dwarves.

Usually, it was the miners who conducted the first refinement of the ore. They would use their hammers to break lumps of rock into small fragments, then grind these even smaller before heating the rock to immense temperatures in huge covered furnaces in order to melt it; the furnace was constructed so that the molten iron could be partly extracted from the slag, or waste material. Once this semirefined material had cooled and hardened, it would be sold throughout the surrounding area for the best price.

A skilled blacksmith would be able to take semirefined ore, and evaluate it, and figure out the best way to make a good sword blade. Ore is different in different regions, containing different trace elements; some of these elements were good for a blade, making it tougher, or they may have enabled the blacksmith to put a slightly harder edge on it, or heat-treat it to a higher

Elven smiths reforged the shards of Narsil; the new sword was named Andúril, Flame of the West.

degree. Ores from other regions would not have made as good a sword, so, if necessary and possible, the blacksmith would mix different ore supplies, welding or twisting different sections together. Access to a good ore supply rendered this process unnecessary; it also made the sword less expensive.

When the blacksmith had bought a quantity of semirefined ore, he would heat up his own, much smaller furnace and begin a further process of refining, this time beating and hammering it to push out any slag residue (this would show up as dark fragments within the glowing core of iron). This process would continue for as long as necessary, depending on the quality of steel he wanted. Iron would become steel when a sufficient quantity of carbon and other minerals was introduced into it during the forging process.

Ore was separated into two grades, the high-grade ore being used for weapons and the low-grade for armor. The blacksmith then repeatedly heated it, hammered it and stretched it out, trying to get as much of the slag out as possible; he would fold the red-hot iron back in on itself, welding it back together, beating it out again, trying to extract as much good molten iron from the mass as possible. This was

The Orcs may have learned their skill with weaponcraft from Sauron himself.

the process now known as folding and stretching. It was principally to refine the iron, to get rid of the impurities and produce a consistent piece of high-quality steel. Once this had been performed enough times the blacksmith would have a piece of steel that was fit for a sword.

From there, making a sword by forging was all about shaping and balancing the blade. All of the real work had been done in the refining. Now the blacksmith would take his piece of steel, heat it, hammer it into a blade shape, form a fuller if needed, which pushed the metal out sideways, and then form down the edges so that in the final grinding stages he could take this rough forged blade and grind it off to get the final shape. In that final grinding he would introduce the taper down to the sword point, while evaluating the flex of the blade and getting the balance correct. He wouldn't want too much weight at the tip because that would make the sword slower, whereas if it was too light the blade would lack effective impact and tire the swordsman who was trying to overcompensate for this. So the smith would put a taper in the blade if possible, thinning the blade so it wasn't too stiff at the tip but stiff enough toward the

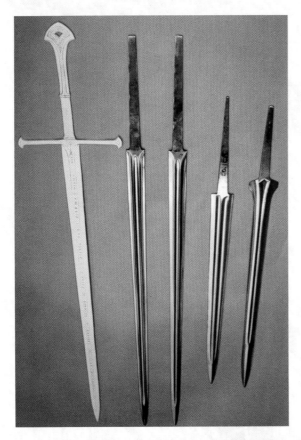

Once the blade had been forged it was ready for the guard, handgrip and pommel to be placed over the tang.

because it has a head out in front that the warrior is trying to propel. A sword relies on speed and slashing power rather than impact, so weight isn't an advantage.

Making the blade light helps the hilt, which has a combination of functions: there is the handgrip, which is shaped to fit in the warrior's fist, and a guard in front between the hand and the blade, which is partly to stop the hand sliding up the blade; it also protects the hand. If an enemy smashed his shield into the warrior's sword arm it wouldn't crack onto his knuckles. If the guard is a wide and crosslike, it stops an enemy blade sliding up and into the warrior's hand. The pommel is a counterweight, but at the same time it has other aspects: it can be used as a bashing weapon, which is where the modern term "pummeling" comes from. The pommel can't be too big; otherwise it would get in the way when the swordsman tried to bend his wrist. If too wide it would stick into his arm, thus forcing the blade out of alignment with his sword arm. So certain shapes can be used and certain shapes cannot. Lastly, there is the decorative function: if the pommel was made of iron it could be put onto the tang and then be decorated with inlays, etching, or jewels; it could even be hollowed out like Narsil if the swordsmith possessed sufficient skill. If the pommel was made of a metal such as bronze there was then the possibility of casting various designs into it by using the "lost wax" process: a complex pommel design could be built in wax, from which a shell would be formed that would then be used to cast it in bronze, giving a perfect reproduction.

hilt so that it would flex evenly. One of the great skills was forming a blade that was as light as possible but as strong as possible and that had a hard sharp edge.

Typically, the blade might be made by one person, and the different fittings made by several other people, because the sword and hilt combined metalwork, jewelry, the wood and leather of the grip and other embellishments. Sometimes one person would do the whole process, but usually the blade-maker would hand the blade to the hilt-maker and he would then start his side of the process. A skilled blade-maker would try to make the blade as light as possible, because for every extra bit of steel in the blade twice that much at least would be needed in the pommel to get the balance working. So any excess in the blade tripled what was in the final sword. Weight isn't an advantage in a sword; the lighter it can be made to do the job, the more effective it becomes. In combat, the sword is meant to be a fast weapon; an axe is slower

A sword has always been a prestigious weapon; it has been a symbol of rank because there's something special about a sword. It is designed only for warfare: whereas a spear or bow can be used for hunting, the sword is one of

Blood would stick to the metal and begin eating into it almost immediately.

the few weapons designed purely to kill. Anyone who owned a sword had demonstrated that he had the money to spend on a weapon that had no real secondary function. While not a utility weapon, it was a very efficient combat weapon; the very fact that you had to draw one meant that you were already in close combat – not an ideal situation – so it needed to have been forged and shaped to the highest possible standard, and well cared for. If your sword failed you for any reason during this stage of combat you would be dead. For this reason, a warrior treated his sword with the same love and respect that he showed to one of his family.

Even with the very best care, a blade would become marked, so no matter how well it was cared for and kept oiled, little spots of hard black corrosion would appear, a form of rust but harder to get out. So over time you would get patches of slight pitting and little grayed areas where this rusting had started; despite being cleaned, it would still be there, like a shadow in the metal. And these areas would keep growing; a blade could be completely covered with gray areas even while being looked after. If the warrior was involved in battle for an extended period he might not be able to look after his blade as he should, so it would succumb to rusting; and if the rain got into his scabbard this might actually produce whole patches of rust on the blade. No doubt these would be cleaned off when possible, but they would still start to chew in. Another enemy of the sword was blood, which was very bad for the blade because it contains iron. If you had dried blood on your blade and then a little moisture got onto it, it would start to rust very quickly. You had to clean any blood off your sword right away if you wished to protect the metal. And that harder type of black rust would have been cutting into the blade anyway, so it was a constant battle against a most difficult enemy. There was the same prob-

lem with steel hilt fittings; the blade would spend most if its life protected by the scabbard, which might have oil in it, but the hilt fittings would be knocked and scratched, and exposed to the elements, leaving them constantly open to attack from rust.

The other major threat to a sword was the physical damage suffered when it was drawn and used in battle. Every time the blade was brought down upon a hard surface, whether metal armor or shield, or even bone, tiny dents and chips would very likely appear in the sharp yet narrow blade edge. Similarly, if two swords came into contact they would not – as is commonly thought – slide smoothly over each other but instead snag, creating further jagged edges that had to be beveled out with a whetstone, gradually reducing the width, strength and ultimately the effectiveness of the blade. Then the warrior would return to the blacksmith and the whole process would begin again.

– From *Third Age Swords and Their Craft*

96

Men of Rohan

THE PEOPLE WHO RODE SOUTH with Eorl into Rohan were part of an ever-expanding population who had originally lived in the wide plains of Rhovanion south of Mirkwood. They were tall for the time, standing on average between five foot ten and six foot two, strongly built and predominantly blond. Their growing numbers led them to migrate first to the Vales of Anduin and then – following the collapse of the Witch-realm of Angmar – to the land north-west of Mirkwood between the Misty Mountains and the Grey Mountains. Yet Rohan proved ideal, its vast rolling plains of grassland allowing them to breed and herd their horses and to establish settlements far and wide across the land.

The culture of Rohan revolved around its horses. Apart from them, the people had little material wealth; their lifestyle was not much above subsistence level. They farmed the land, hunted for all their food and made clothes from animal hides, wool and harvested flax. They mined virtually no ore; instead, they traded with Gondor – horses for ore – taking the semirefined iron ore and smelting it in their modest smithies.

Every man, woman and child in Rohan would have known the value and importance of metal in their lives, from the cooking pots used to nourish them to the swords that protected them. Swords and armor were handed down from father to son, the blade cleaned, sharpened and oiled to prolong its life as much as possible, and the mail repaired with new links in the same way that a shirt was patched and stitched.

There was no tradition of writing in Rohan, so all history, skills and knowledge were handed down orally, parent to child. This

ABOVE *The Men of Rohan journeyed to Mordor itself to defend their freedom.*
LEFT *A painting inspired by one of the Edoras tapestries, showing King Folca hunting a giant boar that would prove to be his nemesis.*

A tapestry of one of the Kings of the Mark, which hung in the Golden Hall.

was as true in the cots of the settlement as it was in the Courts of Edoras, whose walls additionally bore the record of Rohan's history through beautifully illustrated and complex tapestries. The history of a sword was tied to the history of a particular family, and its new recipient would learn as much about its cultural past as he did about his ancestors. This knowledge helped to put iron in the men's hearts as well as in their hand, for the young warrior would be well aware that he had a long and noble tradition to live up to. Although they were not a warfaring society, generations spent defending their settlements from attack had made the Rohan ready and willing to take up arms and give their lives if necessary in the continuing war against Sauron's tyranny.

In the years leading up to the War of the Ring, Gríma Wormtongue's control over King Théoden had grown to such a point that he effectively ruled in the king's name, his dictates enforced by the thugs he had hired as his personal bodyguard. As Saruman was strengthening his army and encroaching on Rohan's northern and western borders, Wormtongue's role was to prevent any military mobilization within the kingdom. With Uruk-hai and Wild Men harrowing the land, each settlement had to rely on its own forces for protection, and with Wormtongue suppressing news of the attacks and dismissing

Early Third Age tapestry depicting Felaróf the meara throwing Léod, father of Eorl, to his doom.

a call to arms, none of the settlements was fully prepared.

Rohan was a hard place to live, even in peace. There were no large cities full of industry and commerce; instead, it was a far more pastoral life. Everything the Rohan did for today was directed toward preparing for tomorrow: growing, reaping and selling crops, and raising cattle to sell and eat. Although under the absolute rule of the king, the people of the outlying settlements were still largely autonomous; many were nomadic, driving their horses, cattle or sheep across the wide plains. Others were localized, especially if they grew wheat or other grain crops, but they were all far-flung and still quite isolated, so every settlement needed to be able to defend itself. As part of their lifestyle, in order to live largely free from the oppressive presence of the king's officials, these farmers and herders and bakers and blacksmiths needed to fight for their freedom, to defend themselves against outlaws and bandits and Orc raiders. This necessity made them tough, suspicious of strangers, but highly adept in reacting quickly to a situation; they maintained regular patrols to protect their homelands, always ready to go out and meet the enemy. Because of Sauron and Saruman's influence, growing numbers of

Orcs were attacking these settlements, so this may explain why Éomer was able to muster two thousand Rohirrim as quickly as he did, and why Théoden had only six thousand of the hoped-for ten thousand when he rode to Gondor. Their loyalty to king and country would have been at its highest even as their losses grew.

THE ROHIRRIM

Known in Gondor as the Riders of Rohan, the Rohirrim were the mounted warriors of Rohan. As is typical with horse cultures, the young people of Rohan first mounted a horse about the same time that they started walking. By the time they were ready to go to war, they were phenomenal riders, completely attuned to the horse, forming a bond so powerful that horse and rider moved and thought as one. If a rider was killed, and the horse became captured, it would pursue freedom or death before it allowed a hostile creature upon it.

RIGHT *When closing in against infantry the Rohirrim would form an impenetrable wall.* BELOW *The trusting bond between horse and rider allowed the Rohirrim to travel in tight columns.*

This cavalry was not a permanent force; rather they were ordinary civilians, herders and trainers who roamed across the wide grasslands with their great herds. Only in times of war were they mustered, as it took many days for word to be spread throughout the kingdom. The basic unit of Riders was called an éored, comprising a particular lord's household or settlement and sworn to his service, and led by a noble or distinguished warrior. Farther afield, an éored would be drawn from the settlement. Its size would vary depending on the nature of the settlement; if it possessed more herders than farmers it would be able to form only a smaller éored from its widely spread riders, unlike the more sedentary agricultural community. With the finest horses in Middle-earth, and with riders who were fully their match, the Rohirrim were the greatest mounted warriors of any age, and there were no infantry units who could withstand them. For this reason, their alliance was greatly prized by Gondor, whose army comprised mainly infantry units.

The Rohirrim were skilled in both light and heavy cavalry attacks and would have adopted a strategy that depended on the size of the opposing force. Against a raiding party of Orcs, they would use a hit and run approach, riding close and firing arrows into the ranks, to try to break morale and force the Orcs to flee; there would be no point in an infantry unit trying to chase them, as the Riders would have outrun them, turned and then repeated the attack. Once the demoralized force chose to retreat, the Riders would chase and harry them, attacking their unprotected backs until all were dead. Of course, on the wide open plains the approaching Rohirrim would have been visible for a long time, and in most instances a show of force was enough to drive off bandits or outlaws. All the Rohirrim needed do was ride up on to a crest, line up with their spears held aloft, and rely on their reputation to drive the enemy off. A physical confrontation would have been the last resort, in order not to risk their horses or themselves. Although they fought as one unit, they were able to disband and still perform at their best without the need to be commanded.

Against a more determined or more numerous foe, the Rohirrim would still use the bow as a principal weapon – the range weapon always formed the first stage of the combat strategy – to try to thin the enemy ranks and create gaps in their line. (The horses weren't stupid and would have shied away from charging into a solid line of defenders. Also, no sensible commander would have ordered a charge into a line of spears, unless the enemy was disordered.) Once a breach was made, the Rohirrim would form a tight phalanx and charge in using their heavy ash spears; these they would hold as lances until they broke through the front ranks, then throw them at short range in the enemy's midst. Some commanders may have held a separate unit of archers off to the side to continue peppering the enemy while the lancers rode toward them. The combination of the thunderous noise and the sight of these powerful beasts and their riders bearing down upon an infantry defense would have struck fear into enemy hearts; the Rohirrim would have towered above them, out of reach of enemy blows but perfectly equipped to drive their spears into flesh. This charge would punch through the defensive ranks, splitting them to create a big gap; an enemy divided in this way would lose its sense of security as part of a larger whole, further weakening their resolve to fight. In the meantime, the Riders would pass through the ranks of defenders, wheel around and ride into their unprotected rear with swords and axes drawn ready to hack down upon enemy heads. So the training for every rider was to use the bow first, then the lance, throw the lance, then draw the sword and start cleaving. This strategy had been ingrained into them from the start; it had worked for centuries and would

The Royal Guard were on constant duty guarding the entrance to the Golden Hall of Meduseld.

serve them well in the greatest battle of the War of the Ring, when they rode onto the Pelennor Fields.

ROYAL GUARD

These men, numbering between thirty and fifty in Théoden's time, were the elite warriors in Rohan, handpicked for their skill and particular loyalty. As the king and his family's personal guard, they were equipped out of the royal purse. (A parsimonious ruler was a poorly protected one, which could quickly result in his being a dead one.) This meant that the quality of their armor and weaponry was second only to that of the monarchy, and they were well-trained with a full range of weapons. The Royal Guard possessed the only unified armor among the Rohan warriors, consisting of a sleeveless, full-length scale hauberk that was effective on foot and on horse, and a helmet featuring a visor with cutouts for the eyes,

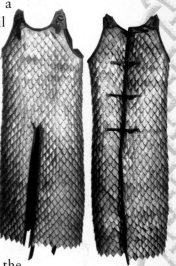

cheek-plates and a tall metal crest of a horse's head from which flowed a mane of horsehair; a mail aventail was riveted inside the back of the helmet's skull. The guards additionally wore steel vambraces and pauldrons overworked with leather, which were strapped to the arms, and a steel collar; both the helmet and collar were extensively worked in bronze. A fine wool cloak dyed green and edged with a red and gold pattern was attached to the leather hems of the hauberk with circular bronze brooches featuring the sun device. The leather of the scabbard and the handgrip was dyed the same green as the cloak.

WEAPONS

The primary consideration with weaponry when on a horse was reach; when not using his primary weapon, the bow, the Rider needed to be able to reach down and strike at his foe. Despite a horse's great speed when moving forward, it was not especially maneuverable in a melee, so having a long reach would allow the Rider to hack and slash at the enemy on each flank.

Bow

Although the bow was the Rohan's primary weapon it was not sophisticated; it was a short bow made from a single piece of wood. It was probably heated, slightly bent and shaped into a subtle curve, but this simple design would not have produced a particularly powerful bow, giving an effective range of about only 125 yards. The arrows were short, as the draw distance was not great, and the tips featured the same cutout seen in the spearheads, which was a cultural motif of Rohan. This feature may have been dictated by two things: the metal being in short supply and the need to cut down on the weight when carrying them. The cutouts would not have enabled the arrows to travel farther; the Rohan were more interested in having their arrows create big wounds that would bleed a lot, so by removing some of the mass of metal they could increase the surface area of the arrowhead while keeping the weight the same. Unique among all arrows in Middle-earth, the flights were made of leather; perhaps the Rohan's skill with a bow was not up to catching the birds in the first place. The quiver was all leather with an internal canvas bag, and could be bound tighter or wider depending on the number of arrows in it. The drawstring bag kept the arrows dry and further stopped them from moving around when the warrior was on horseback. These two levels of security allowed for the quiver to be slung across the back or hung down by the saddle. As the bows did not have an arrow rest, the Rohan wore leather gloves to protect the fingers that drew the string as well as the bow hand from the snap of the string.

Spear

The spear was the secondary weapon for the Riders, but was the primary charging weapon, as it projected a sharp point beyond the front of the horse and so could be used both as a lance, to exploit any weakness in the defensive line, and as a short-range throwing weapon. The spear was made of ash and stood approximately nine feet high. Its long tip was made of steel; half its three-foot length was the cutout tip, and the rest was the sheath, which was riveted onto the shaft. This was then bound in leather and swaged with two bronze rings to give a handgrip for pulling the spear out after a kill. The combination of the steel tip, the heavy weight of the two inch thick shaft and the forward momentum when the spear was thrown from a moving horse meant that it would penetrate any defense, whether armored or not, often passing through into the next rank.

Sword

The most distinctive feature of a Rohan sword was that it generally did not have a fuller; instead it was milled so that it had a slightly concave diamond-shaped cross-section. The wide blade was between twenty-eight and thirty inches in length and tapered very quickly

to a rounded point. The hilt was just long enough for one hand to grip it, and the relatively large guard and pommel were both rounded; this mirrored the design of the Rohan shield and allowed the greatest area for embellishment, mostly with sun or horse motifs. As there was no state-funded army as such, apart from the Royal Guard, the sword would become a family piece and so was well cared for. Successive generations would add ever more elaborate engravings to the guard and pommel, but the blade would begin to show its age, becoming narrower and weaker as chips gained in combat were beveled out with a whetstone, reducing the width until eventually the swordsman or his family would need to trade goods in order to acquire ore for a new blade or commission the local blacksmith to make one.

The Rohan used the sword in a downward slashing motion: when they were mounted this was the only way it could be used, but it also suited their strong-armed and less sophisticated fighting style when they were on foot.

Axe

In addition to the sword, the Rohan carried a light axe, which was used on foot and on horseback. It was about three feet long, with a relatively small head whose blade curved up toward the shaft. The high value of metal meant that spear and arrow tips would have been a priority, followed by swords and armor, then by other weapons. The axe was carried on a belt loop, ready to be drawn in close combat against unmounted opponents and used to hack down upon their heads. It could also be thrown, but the warrior would then run the risk of having it thrown back at him. Examples have been discovered that feature extensive bronze engraving on the blade; such beautiful work was probably produced by one of the Royal Guard in Edoras.

Armor

Although they well knew the importance of metal armor, the Rohan were probably not as fond of it as the Dwarves or Gondorians were, because it placed an extra burden of weight upon their horse and because it wasn't a true reflection of them or their horse culture. This

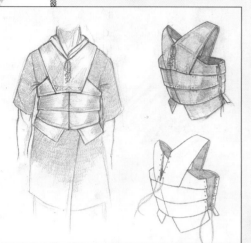

may explain why they faced their cuirasses and pauldrons with leather, which they glued onto the metal shell to give the armor more of their own cultural flavor. The leather did not give any greater protection, but it did help create a thing of beauty. This adornment was found only on the armor worn by the royal family and the Royal Guard, because only at the Courts of Edoras was there time to perform this detailed work, cutting and engraving the leather into complex and beautiful embellishments to imbue it with story and history. Apart from the Royal Guard, the warriors of Rohan were con-scripted from regional clans, and each region would have its own slight variation in armor, as did the families of a clan or settlement. The level of protection was entirely dependent on their wealth and access to materials. Typical items found among an ordinary Rohan armory were simple helmets consisting of a steel skull with a bronze crest in the shape of a horse's head, and cuirasses made of wide, boiled-leather strips that had been glued and riveted together and tightened with rawhide points at the shield-arm side and breastbone. If the Rohan warrior did not possess a helmet it is likely that

he would wear a mail coif that extended into a collar; the coif would usually feature an internal leather or padded canvas skull to help absorb any blow and make it more comfort-able for the wearer. Other than these, they probably wore their ordinary rough woolen tunic and hose, and a heavier woolen cloak.

The Rohan favored mail instead of plate because it required less metal, was more flexible and was lighter when they were on horse-back, reducing the strain on the horse. After several generations, there would have been as many new links in a hauberk as original ones, but essentially it would have been the same item. A mail hauberk was something that could have been repaired almost like a fishing net, the work being done in the home or at the settlement's small smithy, which also would have been used to make horseshoes and other implements. The great advantage with mail was that the maker didn't need to be a skilled armorer in order to produce links that kept the mail serviceable. To a certain degree, this was also true of scale mail, such as that worn by the Royal Guard, because it didn't involve smithing elaborate pieces of metal; it was still a case of forming small, modular pieces that were, on average, easier to make. So even though a typical warrior was unable to make a full suit of mail, he probably could have repaired one.

SHIELD

Rohan shields were made of thin planks of wood that were glued and nailed together in layers running in different directions, and they were often covered in leather skins, which were first cured in vegetable tans so they wouldn't rot. The leather would be soaked in water to soften it so that it could be stretched and fixed using metal pins; then glue would be applied, which was probably neat's foot oil derived from hooves. This was smeared on around the edges, and the leather then additionally secured with metal pins. Once the glue was dried, the pins could be removed. The leather wouldn't necessarily strengthen the shield, for example when taking a direct blow from a sword, but it would hold the shield together if the wood had broken inside and started to come to pieces. However, the leather would need replacing fairly regularly once it had taken knocks in battle. The shield was circular in shape, in order to protect both horse and rider when on the move; any square or sharp edge would have the potential to cut the horse, and this might cause infection or, worse, cause the horse to buck and throw the rider to his doom. Unlike Gondorian shields, it featured an iron bar that was riveted to the back of the shield; this was used as a handgrip, with the fist sitting inside the boss; the boss was big enough so that the warrior could fit his whole fist into it while still keeping it a safe distance from the inside edge of the boss. Gripping the middle of the shield in this way gave the warrior the best ability to counter any angular blow that might twist the shield. The only metal feature was the boss and its handgrip; because of the value of metal to the Rohan, a shield that had been damaged in battle would be recovered wherever possible so that its boss could be removed and put into another shield. The Rohan would often decorate their shields by painting icons of the sun or stylized images of the *mearas*, the race of powerful and intelligent horses that were herded, ridden and revered by the Rohan.

King Théoden

T HÉODEN KING [TA 2948 – 3019], son of Thengel, was the seventeenth king of Rohan. In that country everything revolved around the king, so he needed to possess a powerful and decisive personality, have a strong character and be highly charismatic. Although Théoden had suffered cruelly under the sorcerous yoke of Saruman and Wormtongue's treachery, he had the strength following his liberation by Gandalf to once again become the king his people needed him to be. He kept the majority of the people of Edoras alive by taking them to Helm's Deep, then mustered six thousand Rohirrim to the aid of Gondor, leading this massive cavalry charge as they ploughed into the Orc army. It is said that Théoden outpaced his Royal Guard in his eagerness to reach the Orcs, and his battle fury was terrible to behold. Many fell under his sword before he was attacked by the Witch-king, who dropped out of the sky on his fell beast, killing both Théoden and his beloved horse, Snowmane.

ABOVE *King Théoden led six thousand of his Rohirrim against ten times their number of Orcs.*
RIGHT *The white horse was an emblem of the Royal House.*

SWORD

Herugrim was the name of the king's sword, and it was a noble weapon. Many kings before Théoden had wielded this blade in battle, and many enemies had it slain, including Orcs, Dunlendings, Uruk-hai and Wargs. In appearance it was similar to a standard Rohan sword, being single-handed and measuring about three feet in length; its fullered blade was undecorated, whereas the guard and pommel were ornate indeed; the guard was crafted in the likeness of two horses' heads touching and was made of bronze, as was the large pommel. Herugrim's scabbard was wooden, covered in red leather and featured an ornate bronze chape that complemented the ancient sword. Because Théoden was left-handed, Herugrim was worn on the king's right side.

ARMOR

As with all kings before him, when Théoden was first crowned the royal armorers would have made for him a new suit of armor, using the finest materials and devoting many weeks to the fashioning of something worthy of the king. Instead of steel, the armor was made of solid bronze and was extensively faced with black-dyed leather, all carved with Rohan motifs such as horses, suns and swirls that suggested the flowing movement of the mearas at full gallop. Théoden wore a cuirass, to which was attached tassets and five-piece pauldrons; he additionally wore vambraces and greaves, and a long skirt of steel leaf-mail that was belted around the waist. His steel and bronze helmet featured a bronze noseguard and cheek-plates, and was additionally decorated with copper and tiny details of precious black enamel; the horse crest was solid bronze, and instead of mail the aventail was formed from three lames of boiled leather that were riveted to the skull.

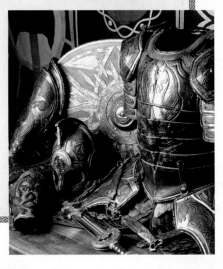

SHIELD

Théoden's shield was larger than a normal Rohan shield and was oval where the others were round. The most likely reason for this difference was that, when held aloft in battle when Théoden was astride Snowmane, it would have served as a recognizable rallying point for his soldiers. The larger surface area also gave greater protection to the king, something the Rohan would be glad to know. The shield was covered in green leather and lavishly decorated on its outer side in bronze with the image of the sun; around the boss was a hunting scene showing one of the king's ancestors and his court pursuing wild boar. Like Herugrim, this shield had probably been carried by a number of kings before Théoden, thus the color was different from that of his armor.

Éomer

ÉOMER [TA 2991 – FO 63] SON OF ÉOMUND, Chief Marshal of the Mark, was nephew to King Théoden and, despite being only twenty-seven at the time of the War of the Ring, was Third Marshal of the Riddermark. After the mortally wounded Théodred was poisoned by Wormtongue, Éomer also became heir to the king. He was tall, strong and possessed of great passion; in battle he was said to have been as fierce as any Orc and as powerful as an Uruk. The loyalty of the men of his éored was absolute, and they were chiefly responsible for limiting the damage caused by Saruman's Uruk-hai during Wormtongue's usurpation.

Éomer was the only one to openly challenge the word of Wormtongue. He had realized that Saruman's white hand was upon every misdeed committed against Rohan and so Rohan must ride against the raiders before the trickle became a flood. Wormtongue banished Éomer from the kingdom, fearing people would soon begin to take heed, so he was forced to ride north with his éored, under pain of death if he ever returned. Ignoring this threat, he visited every settlement he could find, gathering to him many Riders, all of whom were still loyal to the king and ready to ride back to Edoras to oust Wormtongue the usurper. He was eventually intercepted by Gandalf riding Shadowfax, who told him the king would need his aid at Helm's Deep. At this time Éomer is said to have had nearly two thousand Riders with him, and their numbers swelled as they rode southwest to the ancient refuge; although perhaps only a fifth of the total number of Riders in Rohan, they proved sufficient to drive the Uruk army back into the waiting branches of the Hourns. At the Battle of the Pelennor Fields Éomer led one of the companies of Rohirrim against the Mordor host, and when Théoden was slain by the Witch-king he became eighteenth king of Rohan. He accompanied Aragorn to the Black Gate of Mordor, leading the remaining Rohirrim warriors to a certain but noble doom. Yet when Sauron was overthrown he was able to return to the Riddermark, after reaffirming the Oath of Allegiance between Rohan and Gondor.

Éomer commanded one of three companies of Rohirrim at the Pelennor Fields.

WEAPONS

Éomer carried a standard Rohan lance with him when riding with his éored, and he fought with just a sword when in close combat. Éomer's sword was named Gúthwine, and was the  same length as most Rohan blades, being about twenty-eight inches from guard to tip. Like Théoden's sword, the blade was fullered, and the guard and pommel were made from solid bronze. The beautiful guard was fashioned, like all of Théoden's house, to resemble two horses; in Éomer's case they were skillfully crafted so that they reared on either side of the blade. The scabbard hung from a suspension system and was adorned with a heavily engraved bronze locket and chape.

ARMOR

Éomer was a warrior through and through, and he protected himself with a full suit of armor. Over his leather tunic and woolen hose he wore the following: a mail skirt, then a long skirt of leaf-mail belted at the waist, a mail shirt that hung below the waist, and a steel cuirass heavily faced with engraved red leather that was tightly strapped at the sides. On his arms he wore steel pauldrons and vambraces, and over his tall leather boots full greaves that went from ankle to knee; all were similarly faced with red leather. This extensive protection more than compensated for the fact that Éomer carried no shield. His helmet would have been instantly recognizable on the battlefield: made of polished steel and bronze, with long cheek-plates, and engraved with the sun icon on the front, its tall conical shape marked it out as different. And with its long bronze nose-guard in the shape of a horse and its tall crest of long pale horsehair that flowed down his back like a real mane, it would have been like a banner itself, enabling all Rohan warriors to locate Éomer in the midst of a melee. The helmet also featured precious jewels and enameling, as befitting his royal status.

Éowyn

ALONG WITH HER BROTHER, Éomer, Éowyn [TA 2995 – FO ?] was raised in Edoras following the early death of her mother and father. Her childhood was cut short when she was required to look after her uncle, King Théoden, fast declining under Saruman and Wormtongue's increasing control. Like many Rohan women of noble birth, she trained to be a Shield-maiden and was considered the equal if not the better of many of the men with a sword. Idealistic, spirited, brave, high-minded, and slightly lonely, she was only twenty-three at the time of the War of the Ring and fell in love with Lord Aragorn when he came to Edoras with other members of the Fellowship in TA 3019. When she realized that her love was doomed to be unrequited she determined to find an honorable death on the field of battle. Although sent to the Glittering Caves by her uncle at the Battle of Helm's Deep, she fought bravely, killing many Uruk-hai as she protected the refugees who were hiding there. Later, and against her uncle's wishes, she rode in disguise with the Rohirrim to the Pelennor Fields, taking the hobbit Merry with her. Both achieved a supreme act of heroism when they rode to the defense of their fallen king, and succeeded in slaying the Witch-king. (This fulfilled an ancient and enigmatic prophecy, which said that he could never be killed by the hands of Men.) In striking the killing blow, Éowyn took a grievous injury, but she was subsequently healed by King Elessar. In the Houses of Healing she finally relinquished all dreams of battlefield glory, and found love in the arms of Faramir, whom she wed, living with him until the end of their days in the fair land of Ithilien.

LEFT *Fully trained as a Shield-maiden, Éowyn was the equal of any man in combat.*
ABOVE *She was determined to find glory on the battlefield, even at the cost of her life.*

Weapons

As a shield-maiden Éowyn carried a full-sized sword, which measured nearly three feet in length, including the hilt. The beautiful bronze guard and pommel were styled in honor of

the mearas, and the handgrip featured a raised middle section of three bronze rings, presumably to improve the grip of Éowyn's small hand upon the sword. Like other royal swords, the blade's wide fuller ran along three-quarters of its length. Its scabbard was suspended from a shoulder-harness suspension system so that the sword hung almost horizontally, allowing Éowyn to draw it very quickly. When riding into battle the petite warrior carried with her a full-sized lance that had a red leather handgrip behind the blade, a mark of nobility that escaped the attention of her fellow Rohirrim.

Armor

The armor that Éowyn wore to the Pelennor Fields was of regular design and manufacture, perhaps indicating that it was gathered from the Edoras armory in a hurry. She wore a full mail hauberk over her woolen dress, then added a cuirass of boiled leather laced up the front with rawhide points. Attached to the cuirass by straps were leather tassets. Éowyn's shield was also of standard issue. Her helmet was perhaps chosen with more care, as she would have needed something that obscured all of her distinctive features, so it provided full cheek, nose and eye protection, and a mail aventail covered Éowyn's hair even as it protected her neck.

Legolas

LEGOLAS GREENLEAF WAS A PRINCE OF THE MIRKWOOD ELVES, the scion of a noble Elven family. His grandfather was Oropher, who fought and fell with Gil-galad during the Last Alliance, and his father was Thranduil, the Elvenking who imprisoned the thirteen Dwarves that accompanied Bilbo on the quest to the Lonely Mountain. It is therefore possible that Legolas would have been present at the king's court when Bilbo was there, and more than likely that Gimli would not have forgotten that the Elf's father had so ill-treated his own.

Curiously, accounts differ as to his appearance, some saying that he had brown hair and green eyes, others that he was blond with blue eyes; most suggested that he stood around six feet tall. However, all agree that he was one of the finest marksmen with a bow in all Middle-earth, able to react with lightning speed and deadly accuracy, to the great benefit of the Fellowship of the Ring.

As with his friend Gimli the Dwarf, little is known of Legolas's deeds before he went to Rivendell as emissary of the Silvan Elves of Mirkwood; it is likely that as prince of that realm, he had led the defense of its borders for many years, honing his skills with a bow at the expense of many Orc lives. Evidently he had never traveled from the great Wood, as his travels with the Fellowship took him for the first time to Lothlórien, the Golden Wood of his kin ruled by Galadriel and Celeborn, where he gazed upon those who had seen the Blessed Realm of the Undying Lands. Here, his fighting ability was increased significantly when he was given a specially made Lórien bow, together with a quiver and many bundles of

ABOVE *Legolas was already millennia old at the time of the War of the Ring.*
LEFT *His skill with a bow was said to be unmatched.*

The draw of the Lórien bow was huge, requiring great strength to draw it fully.

in the Battle of the Pelennor Fields alongside Gimli with bow and knife, Legolas journeyed back to the Glittering Caves, where he beheld a wonder to surpass even his own father's subterranean palace. Yet on his homeward journey he ventured near the coastline and heard for the first time the call of the sea. This awoke in Legolas the deep yearning of his people to sail into the Undying Lands, and eventually he took ship from the Grey Havens, taking with him the now-frail Dwarf who had been his bravest comrade and his truest friend.

arrows; the bow was large and much more powerful than his Mirkwood bow and the arrows were larger: these would have proved invaluable against the Uruk-hai. After fighting

Bows

Legolas carried with him a bow of dark wood, probably yew, that he had made in his youth in Mirkwood. It was outwardly simple in construction, carved from a single piece of wood in the style of the Númenórean longbows, but engraved in gold with a delicate pattern of ivy that twined along both limbs. Legolas spent most of his time firing the bow from within the tree canopy, so it was not especially long, standing sixty inches tall when strung. But it was very powerful and could easily fire an arrow 250 yards with deadly force, although it is likely that within the thick canopy of Mirkwood he was usually much closer than this when out hunting the enemy. The Mirkwood arrows were thirty inches long, sturdy enough to cope with the poundage, and stained dark brown to match the bow. They had long hunting points with very narrow tips, rather like a bodkins, for maximum penetration of armor and flesh. The green flights almost certainly came from pheasant or other game birds that lived in the surrounding woods, and the nocks were hand-carved. They were housed in a wooden quiver that had been dyed and coated in resin to give it a deep lustrous sheen, then further enhanced with thick golden scrollwork around the mouth of the quiver.

The bow given to Legolas in Lórien was a wondrous piece of craftsmanship; apparently formed from a single piece of mallorn heartwood, it had been skillfully carved so that it appeared to be covered with leaves and vines, all in a slightly paler wood than the stave. The bow stood about sixty-eight inches high when strung and reputedly could send an arrow 400 yards with great accuracy; if the rumors are true that its string was blessed with a strand of hair from Lady Galadriel herself, then this claim may indeed be true. Some quality of the mallorn wood kept its draw at around 150 pounds, similar to that of the Mirkwood bow despite its greater length and range. When not carried in the hand, the bow could be stored in a leather holster that was tied to the quiver suspension system with rawhide points. The arrows were about forty inches long and slightly thinner than the Mirkwood arrows in order to keep the weight down. Their green-gold flights were of turkey feathers that had been trimmed into a diamond shape, their shafts dyed sage green. The long-sleeved steel tips were of the mallorn-leaf design that ensured maximum wound-size and damage. Because of the high poundage, the nocks were reinforced with either bone or a special kind of flint found only in the Silverlode. The Lórien quiver was wood with a leather covering; a beautiful design of a peacock, a rare bird in Middle-earth, had been inlaid in gold, and the mouth had been fitted with a locket of gold. It held approximately two dozen arrows and was attached to a suspension system that was belted tightly around the shoulders and torso to prevent any movement while traveling or fighting. With such a precise and fast method of reaching back over his shoulder for an arrow, Legolas needed to know that they were exactly where he expected them to be.

WHITE KNIVES

Attached by rawhide straps to his bow holster and quiver suspension system were two leather scabbards, each containing a long knife. These were known as White Knives, probably because of the pearlescent scabbards, and were a little under two feet in length; the handle was about eight inches long, inlaid with the iconic Elven vine scroll, and curved in the same way as Elrond's sword, Hadhafang, to resemble a living shoot. Like that famous sword, the knives had a bronze guard and pommel fitted diagonally onto the tang, matching the shape of the handgrip exactly so that no metal protruded. The sixteen-inch blade was made from the finest-grade steel, heavily etched and engraved with brass in a complex pattern of scrollwork and vines. Each knife was honed only on the downward side, and the point was sharply tapered, allowing Legolas to use it in fast, slashing strokes and short stabbing motions. As he did

not carry a sword (except when he rode out with Théoden and Aragorn at Helm's Deep and would have needed to be able to reach the unmounted Uruk-hai), Legolas would have relied on hand and body speed to keep him from harm as he simultaneously wielded both blades in a dual whirling attack. There is no record of him using just one knife, so it can be reasonably be assumed that Legolas was ambidextrous.

ARMOR

It is said that apart from the two leather bracers, Legolas wore armor only once in his life, when he readied himself for battle at Helm's Deep. Like his Sindarin kin he knew that there would be brutal close-quarter fighting that would not allow any room to maneuver, so his concession to safety was to wear eight-lamed pauldrons of tough boiled leather that were strapped around his arms and across his chest. The lames were riveted together but probably still allowed him sufficient mobility; the fourth, sixth and eight lames were engraved with a Rohan motif. There was no opportunity for Legolas to similarly prepare himself before the Battle of the Pelennor Fields, so the Elf entered the fray wearing only his customary traveling outfit of embroidered pale blue silk shirt, soft gray-green woolen hose, tall suede boots shaped liked overlapping leaves and decorated with the plant motif and a double-layered suede jerkin; the under-layer was khaki-green and the slightly thicker outer layer was brown, and both were cut into petal shapes so that it resembled a flower bud. The tunic was cut to just below the waist and to the elbows, and was split up the sides so that it did not restrict his movements. Over this was worn the cloak given to him in Lórien, which was pinned to the tunic with a silver leaf brooch.

Elves of Lothlórien

THE SO-CALLED DARK YEARS of Sauron's dominion over much of Middle-earth during the Second Age had achieved his aim of eradicating the Eldar in a more subtle way than originally intended: by causing a shadow of foreboding to fall on the hearts of many of the Elves. The Middle-earth that they had loved was no more, and despite the costly battle of the Last Alliance Sauron had been allowed to survive. Furthermore, the race of Men, from whom had come the one who had allowed this to happen, were increasing in numbers and prominence, imposing their will and shaping the land to their own design. The Elves realized that the world was changing, that their time as custodians of Middle-earth was drawing to a close, whether the fate of the Ring-bearer and his quest was successful or not. Many decided to take ship into the west: for those of the first-born race, the Third Age heralded the fading years of the Elves, an autumn in their lives.

This awareness that it was the autumn of their time in Middle-earth flowed through into the design of their armor. Whereas before the gold of their metals had been infused with the green of springtime and the lames of their pauldrons were fat and full like a new bud, now the armor was burnished with the coppers and auburns of late harvest and the setting sun, the buds gone and the leaves now withered and brown.

Yet despite this melancholic acceptance that the time of departure was near, there were

RIGHT *None of the Moria Orcs pursuing the Fellowship left Lórien alive.*
BELOW *The Elves, led by Haldir, carried Galadriel's banner to Helm's Deep.*

The longbows of the Galadhrim accounted for hundreds of Uruk-hai deaths.

still some who were prepared to honor the old alliance between Men and Elves. Their principal advocate was Haldir of Lothlórien, who was one of the most senior wardens guarding the Golden Wood from attack. He persuaded the diffident Galadriel and Celeborn – with support from Elrond, even though many of the Elves of Rivendell, including his beloved Arwen, were departing for the Gray Havens – that the Men of Rohan, and the race of Men in general, should not be abandoned in their hour of need. With their permission, Haldir rallied two hundred of the Elves of Lothlórien to join him, and together they marched to Helm's Deep bearing the banners of their Lady Galadriel, arriving just ahead of the approaching Uruk-hai army. Few within the ancient stronghold understood the immensity of the sacrifice they were making:

LEFT *Elven banner featuring Galadriel's heraldic device.*
RIGHT *Helm's Deep represented the single greatest loss for the Galadhrim during the Third Age.*

they had forfeited the chance of eternal bliss in the Undying Lands to march to almost certain death, aiding the very people who were changing the face of their beloved Middle-earth.

Because this would be a battle fought at close quarters without the benefit of trees to protect them, the Elves wore their finely worked armor and helmets and took with them their longbows and swords. The reasons for their not taking shields are many and various: first, because they were Galadhrim, or Tree-elves, a shield was unnecessary and burdensome, especially as most of their attacks came from within the tree canopy; a shield would have proved tiring to carry over a long

distance without rest, and the urgent need of the Rohan would not have allowed for rest; the battlements of Helm's Deep would have provided significant protection; and, last, the combination of their weapons of choice and their fighting style would not have allowed for carrying a shield as well – the Elven sword was wielded two-handed, as was the bow.

The Elves' involvement in the defense of the Hornburg proved critical in delaying the enemy; without their superior archery and sword skills, the Uruks would have quickly overrun the Rohan defenses and killed the women and children long before Gandalf, Éomer and the two thousand mounted Rohirrim warriors arrived.

Under Aragorn's leadership, the two hundred Elves killed ten times that number of Uruk-hai soldiers, using their extraordinary ability with a bow to dispatch many of the armored soldiers with a well-placed arrow. But the price they paid was high indeed: none of the Elves who left Lothlórien, including Haldir, ever returned to accompany their kin on that final journey to the Undying Lands. They were buried by the Men of Rohan with honor in the land of their allies.

BOW

The bows of the Galadhrim were probably the most beautiful in all Middle-earth, and certainly the most powerful; they were made from the legendary mallorn trees that grew only in the Golden Wood of Lórien. The heartwood of these trees was silvery white in color, but took on a rich golden color when left to dry before being gradually heated and bent into the strong, recurved lines unique to the Wood-elves. The seven-foot stave was sealed with mallorn resin and gilded in an elegant embossed pattern of twining golden leaves on either side of the leather handgrip; the curved ends of the stave were gilded and bore a spur, but the nock was located a few inches farther in. The length of the bow meant that it could never be fully drawn, but the Elves would still pull the string back beyond the eye rather than up to it. This required a huge amount of individual strength and years of training as the bows would have had a draw of more than two hundred pounds. It is said that the strings of the bows carried within them a single strand of Elven hair, to give greater strength and power to the arrow's flight. The combination of the inherent power of the mallorn wood and the energy generated from the curves in each arm of the bow meant that the Galadhrim could send an arrow with pinpoint accuracy across enormous distances, perhaps a quarter of a mile or more.

The pale arrows were almost four feet long, made from unstained ash or occasionally mallorn shoots, with long broad-headed tips made of gold, which extended into a long sleeve that gave greater stability. The barbs gave the tips the subtle appearance of a

mallorn leaf and were used as cutting edges to tear into the enemy; they were lethal against all targets, whether armored or not. The flights were long white goose or swan feathers, and these were skillfully tied to the shaft in a spiral pattern with a single cork-screwing loop of gold wire. Lórien arrows were the only ones at that time to employ a spiral fletching, so it can be assumed that the Elves were unique in discovering that an arrow fired with a spiraling flight is much more accurate than a normal one. To withstand the force generated by these powerful bows, the nocks were reinforced with a transverse piece of deer antler so that the wood did not shatter when the string was released.

The design of the quiver, like that of the sword, differed little from that used almost three thousand years before; it was leather, stood roughly half the length of the arrows, and its mouth resembled two overlapping leaves. However, the Elves of Lórien did embellish them with the same embossed gold vine pattern found on all their armor.

SWORD

The sword carried by the Elves of Lórien differed little from that carried by their Noldorin kin during the Last Alliance. It can therefore be assumed that the design had already reached its pinnacle in the Second Age, and was merely faithfully reproduced whenever a new sword was required. Of course, some of the

Elves that marched to Helm's Deep may have had kin who fought against Sauron's army, and so might have inherited the weapon when that family member took ship to the Undying Lands. As has been said before, the five-foot sword was half blade and half handgrip: the blade was relatively wide given its length, sharp only along the lower edge and with more weight in the top of the blade than near the cutting edge – it was fullered along the entire length of the top part of the blade. The cutting edge curved up to meet the tip, rather than tapering like a normal sword, partly to keep the blade strong along its entire length and partly to extend the cutting edge. The Elves kept both hands on the handgrip, one at each end, and swung the sword in a whirling motion: this motion meant that the tip, which was the fastest-moving part of the blade, would have been scything into the Elves' enemy, so it had to be able to withstand the impact of hitting armor at high speed.

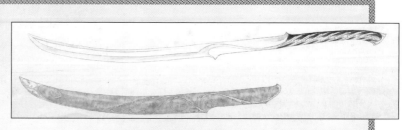

Haldir's sword is reported to have been similar in shape to Hadhafang, but larger and thicker in the blade. Although it bore no runes down the blade, it did have an inset, a curving flower-bud detail that grew into the fuller.

The scabbard of the Elven swords was the twin of them in terms of beauty; made from the trees of the Golden Wood, it was a deep burnished honey color, with gold tengwar patterns etched along its length. It seems to have been attached to the rig that held the quiver as well as to the belt that went around the warrior's waist; like the arrows, it was long and so was worn on the back, being drawn over the shoulder rather than across the body. The usual configuration meant that an Elf would reach over his right shoulder for an arrow and over his left for his sword.

Armor

It can be assumed that during the many thousands of years that the Elves spent living together in Middle-earth they reworked and refined their craft, working toward a state of perceived perfection, while also developing new styles of expression within all that they did. The most significant factor behind the changes made in Elven armor between the Second and the Third Ages was that the armor worn at the Last Alliance was of Noldorin design, whereas that worn at Helm's Deep was fashioned by the Sindarin Elves of Lothlórien. As has already been said, Third Age Elven armor reflected the autumnal themes and hues seen in nature – the coppers and browns and rich golds – as opposed to the greens and yellow-golds of spring, or rebirth, found in the earlier pieces.

Before marching to Helm's Deep the Elves put on their steel battle armor, for they knew that there would likely be hand-to-hand fighting and, since they did not carry shields, their bodies would be exposed to attack. Over their normal traveling clothes they wore a hauberk of very fine gold, leaf-shaped mail with long sleeves, which went into a knee-length skirt of metallic silk that had been painstakingly embroidered to give it a pattern of row upon row of tiny leaf-shapes. Both hauberk and skirt gave the appearance of a carpet of leaves fallen from the

tree, nearing the end of their natural cycle. Unlike the Noldorin armor, the gold-plated steel cuirass and fauld were separate. The cuirass represented the very pinnacle of armor design: it was like a fan in that it featured a hinge point at the breastbone that allowed the lames on each side to move over one another as the soldier drew his arrows and sword, and as he spun and twisted in combat. This hinge point was decorated with a badge that had the Elf's house enameled on it (*left*).

Each lame was slightly curved to represent a fallen leaf, with the veins on the underside of the leaf now exposed; trailing across all the metal armor was a fine gold filigree representing both delicate vines and the tengwar of the written language, Quenya. In the mind of the Elf this would spiritually strengthen the armor, giving him even more confidence in battle. The fauld consisted of eight lames, and like the cuirass these were linked with leather points to move with the soldier as he did; the design again reflected a fallen leaf. The fauld was attached to the body by a leather belt. To further protect the stomach, the Elves wore a leather tunic between the hauberk and the cuirass. Leather was also used for the gloves and the bracers, which extended over the hands to protect them from the snap of the bowstring. To protect the outside of the arms a steel vambrace was tied over the bracer, and a steel pauldron was strapped to the cuirass and arm. The autumnal theme extended to the helmet, in that its latticed steel gave the appearance of a torn leaf. It flexed when it was put on, fitting snugly around the head to ensure that it stayed

in place during battle; the small curved crest was more decorative than defensive. The last item of protection was a cloak of deep green silk, its long ties passing over the shoulders and back, then tied around the waist; although the cloak was of little use against direct attack, its movement could distract the eye of an attacker, causing him to miss his aim. The Sindarin refinement of the Noldorin design resulted in armor that was the most sophisticated ever to be seen in Middle-earth.

By contrast, the Galadhrim wore simple outfits of suede and soft fabrics when in Lothlórien, because their principal protection came from the trees in which they hid and from which they attacked their enemies. The camouflaging grays, browns and greens meant

they were all but invisible, and their natural stealth and speed made them almost invincible when moving through the canopy. This advantage, together with Celeborn's tactical leadership, proved crucial in repelling three attacks by Sauron's forces that occurred at the time of the Siege of Gondor. The royal guards did wear the leather components of their battle armor, but this was probably more ceremonial than functional, as Galadriel would have sensed any threat entering her domain long before it reached Caras Galadhon.

Uruk-hai

T HE URUK-HAI [tr. from Black Speech: "Orc race"] were a thoroughbred strain of Orcs that were first created by Sauron in the Third Age, by crossing Orcs with Goblin-men, to be used as soldiers against the Free Peoples of Middle-earth. Saruman clearly learned Sauron's methods for making them and copied them to build his own army. The foul craft by which he came to make these creatures is still unknown, although so-called birthing pits discovered in the Fourth Age beneath Isengard have led many to think that Saruman used minerals and other deposits in his caverns to help spawn them under the ground. Whereas no two Orcs were likely to be the same, the Uruk-hai had a more uniform appearance: dark red and black skin, large yellow eyes and long black hair. Each Uruk had strong, straight legs. They stood more than six feet tall, unlike the more stunted Orcs, and crucially did not weaken in daylight. Although they were unafraid of the sun, apparently it still burned their skin, charring it to a dead, ashy black.

TOP *Mordor Uruk-hai were more developed than their Isengard kin.*
ABOVE *So-called birthing pits were discovered beneath Isengard.*
INSET *An artist's impression of Uruks being farmed by Saruman's Orcs.*

There were said to be occasional wild mutations, even among this monstrous race.

The Uruk-hai were created only to serve and fight, never to run; presumably the sigil that they bore all over their bodies was a mark of allegiance – or perhaps, in Saruman's mind, a stamp of ownership – to their master, Saruman of the White Hand. The relationship between the Uruk-hai, who saw themselves as superior to all, and the Orcs who oversaw their spawning and training would therefore have been a volatile one. As with their master, the Uruk-hai's arrogance would prove to be their downfall; from the moment they were spawned they had been told that they were invincible, that they were the fighting Uruk-hai, so any unexpected chink in this armor of self-belief would quickly have led to a shattering of confidence, as can be seen in the events of the Battle of Helm's Deep.

The Uruk-hai were raw fighting talent: powerful, obedient machines. They were brutal, disciplined, single-minded and persistent, and could travel long distances with hardly any rest. Like all creatures in thrall to the Eye, they were also ruthless and terrible, lacking any compassion. With only basic drill training and weapons handling they could be shaped into the ideal, purpose-built army.

According to journals found in Saruman's study, one of the earliest successes among Saruman's first batch of Uruk-hai hatchlings was Lurtz. This Uruk was chosen to lead a group of about one hundred Uruk-hai against the Fellowship, in an effort to recover the Halfling Ring-bearer. Using the palantír, Saruman had located the approximate position of the Fellowship; then he had unleashed the first of his soldiers. This first batch would have had time to grow to full strength and develop their skills. Those that came after may

ABOVE *Uruk banner displaying the White Hand of their master.*
RIGHT *A fanciful artist's impression of Orcs training an Uruk.*
BELOW *Uruks were trained to fight as one, single-mindedly.*

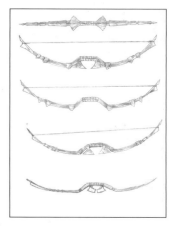

have been weaker because of their enforced, accelerated growth as Saruman hurried to complete his army.

The Uruks trusted with this task would have been a specially equipped elite force; instead of being made of heavy plate, their armor would have been stripped down to just a light leather "traveling armor" so that they could move faster. It would have been crucial not to come into contact with the Rohan, so they could reach their target alive. Both bows and swords have been unearthed at the Amon Hen site, so it seems fair to assume that their training extended to fighting in a more reactive way, whether in a skirmish or on the run, to return fire against the Rohan and to attack the Fellowship from range; yet it may be that the heavy woods surrounding Amon Hen prevented them from employing this first-stage attack, forcing them to engage in close combat. Most of them carried a large recurve composite bow made from springs of steel and wood; its range was limited, but it could

fire a large, heavy arrow because of the huge pull on it. Some accounts have suggested that the pull was as high as three hundred pounds; if true, only an Uruk could have drawn this bow with any accuracy. Because of the use of wood in its construction, the bow would not have survived for long before shattering under the enormous tension. The stave was nearly six feet high; its string was formed from many cords of twine and sinew and was fitted with two intimidating metal blades on the outside that could be used, when an Uruk was out of arrows, as a last strike before the bow was cast aside and the sword was drawn. On his back the Uruk carried a quiver full of thick, black-shafted arrows fletched with Warg fur that had been slicked into fletches using tar. The sword and shield were the same as those carried by the swordsmen at Helm's Deep.

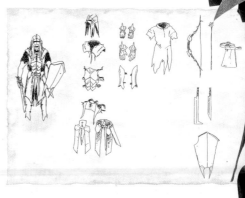

The Uruk raiding party was covered in layers of leather of varying thickness; the helmet had a metal blade for a crest that could be used offensively.

124

The arrows, quiver and bow carried by the traveling Uruk-hai.

Uruks breathed harshly and deeply, and were enormously strong, tense creatures, top-heavy juggernauts with massive chest, neck, shoulder and jaw development. They snarled and grimaced constantly, as if they were in constant pain and their only relief lay in violence. Their gait was like walking uphill on narrow poles, probably because as soon as they were spawned they were locked into heavy plate armor, so there was a perceived sense of crushing weight and momentum to their stride. They had difficulty turning quickly. They probably had limited formal training, just basic drill work, but they were lethal, instinctive fighters, much more dangerous than Orcs. They used their falchions and spiked shields pretty much interchangeably, smashing and bashing. Their defenses were power blocks – no finesse, no deflections, just brutal chops that could bounce an attacking weapon back the way it came. Sometimes they didn't even bother to defend themselves; they just relied on their armor and moved straight into the attack. They would hammer and chop, and occasionally flip their swords around and use the back-spike to pinion an enemy, or gut them with the prongs on their shields.

– From *Cultural Fighting Styles of Middle-earth – A Guidebook*

Before Saruman unleashed his army to crush the kingdom of Rohan, he must have given much thought to how best to accomplish the task. He would not have cared overmuch for the Uruks' survival, because to him they were just fodder, but he could not afford to have them fail; this was his last throw of the dice if he wished to achieve military control of the kingdom. Saruman's greatest asset was his intelligence: long had he lived among the Rohan and much had he learned from his travels and from Wormtongue's spying, so he had a clear understanding of how the Rohen fought and what their weaknesses were. He also realized the shortcomings of his Uruk-hai: they were just simple beasts that could hold only a limited amount of information. This almost certainly explains each Uruk's narrow but well-defined role within the army, depending on which weapon they carried: there were

Ten thousand Uruk soldiers marched south across the Westfold.

tated; the deaths of their commanders would also have confused them, sending them into disarray.

The divisions were broken down into companies that were led by a commander, who kept discipline within the ranks, called the beat when they were marching and gave the orders for where and when to attack. The commander was signified by a distinctive crest of a wide, curving fan of metal that stretched across his helmet, and each commander's crest was unique, with different cutouts and white patterns to enable his troops to pick him out in battle. All of the leaders probably came from the first batch, because only they would have had the intelligence to comprehend and carry out instructions. Saruman's Orcs, however, were more independent thinkers, so he may have permitted them greater knowledge of his plans; the Orcs sent out after Lurtz's raiding party were likely there to ensure that his instructions were carried out properly.

swordsmen, pikesmen, crossbow-men, sappers and the shock-troops, the Berserkers. Each Uruk had been drilled repeatedly, almost from the moment he was spawned, with a brutally simple fighting style relating to a particular weapon or task; to aid this instruction, every weapon had been made to be as intuitive as possible. Their combat strategy would have been simple: a uniform, forward-moving fighting style; because as Saruman never expected his Uruks to retreat, they would not have been trained to fight when moving backward. This short-sightedness meant that once their ranks became broken they would become disorien-

SWORDSMEN

The swordsmen were the main fighting force within the Uruk army. They were equipped with a brutal, one-handed falchion resembling a meat cleaver, which had a spike on the back of the blade for hooking and stabbing. Saruman knew that his Uruks would likely be facing the Riders of the Rohirrim, and so added the spike, which could be used to stab and disembowel their horses, or to hook the cloak of a passing rider, pulling him to the ground; against infantry, the spike could be used to punch through armor. Like every item in the Uruk arsenal, the three-foot weapon was designed along straight lines. The blade was single-edged so the edge could be sharpened quickly on a grindstone: Saruman's Orc-smiths would have been ordered to mass-produce a huge amount of weaponry and armor in just a few weeks, so they would not have been able to alter the shape of the weapon much beyond that of the original

ingot. However, it has been found that the metal was not simply cast iron, so there must have been some beating and working done to avoid its potentially brittle quality. The iron included a small amount of coke: this relative lack of carbon would have made the steel softer,

but a combination of the weight of the weapon – perhaps ten pounds – and the Uruk's brute strength meant that it still could have ripped an opponent's head off. The Uruk sword was a very industrial weapon and very intuitive; when it was given to a primitive, newly spawned Uruk, the Uruk would quickly have grasped how to use it. The only thing required was a great amount of strength, because of the amount of metal in it, and that was something Saruman's Uruk-hai had plenty of, making them deadly effective against the Rohan, even though the men had been fully trained with a sword. One on one, an Uruk-hai would always beat a Rohan soldier.

SHIELDS

The swordsman's large shield offset the weight of the sword and was constructed for a specific dual purpose: protection when used individually in the normal way, and protection collectively when interlocked into a "tortoise," to help the Uruks evade attack from above when assaulting the gates of Helm's Deep with their battering ram. The inclusion of two spikes was both an offensive feature, so that the shield could be used as a stabbing weapon, and a means of linking one shield to another. The straight lines resulted from the simplicity of the industrial design; flat sheets of iron were hammered out quickly to form efficient, functional equipment. The shield's underside was fitted with an iron handgrip and leather enarme so that it sat along the arm; it also had two iron brackets at the back together with a second handgrip. When forming the tortoise each Uruk would insert the spikes of his shield into the brackets of the shield in front; then he would grasp the handgrip at the back of the shield ahead of him, creating a tight-knit protective shell.

127

PIKESMEN

They carried eighteen-foot-long pikes, which were conceived primarily for defending the Uruk ranks against attack from the Rohirrim; a tightly clustered row of pikes meant that the horsemen could be kept at a distance, allowing the crossbow-men to pick them off using the superior range of their weapon. The secondary role of the pike was to help push the siege ladders up when they were being raised against the Deeping Wall. Part of the planned strategy when attacking Helm's Deep would have been to then use the pikes as the front line of attack when the Uruks stormed through the breach in the Deeping Wall. The pikesmen also carried a short sword, which had a beveled, chiseled tip and a narrow blade. It was something that could be easily carried without being an encum-

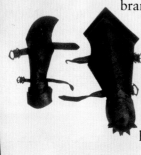

brance. Their leading arm was fitted with a ball-end shield, or manifer, studded with coronels to protect the exposed limb; if the Uruk lost his pike he could use the manifer to bludgeon the enemy, while hacking with the short sword held in his right hand.

CROSSBOW-MEN

The crossbow consisted of a thick steel bow that was held under pressure by a cord of many layers of sinew or twine being drawn back and cocked. The bow was fixed to a beam that had two metal flanges to stabilize and direct the bolt. A trigger sat below the beam, and when this was drawn forward the connecting lever pulled back the cord into a toothed wheel on a central pin, held in place by the trigger. When the trigger was pulled up toward the beam it released the wheel; the wheel spun, releasing the cord and propelling the bolt.

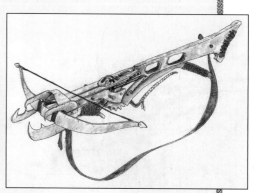

Although the rate of fire was not as good as with a bow it had a set poundage and draw, which meant that it required less training in order to achieve accuracy; with the advent of the crossbow came the first marksmen, because they knew that the second bolt would fly precisely the same distance and to the same location as the first. Because of the great amount of energy generated by this mechanical innovation, the wooden bolts could shatter under the pressure of the cord's impact rather than being released; therefore, they were made of very thick, hard wood and tipped and flighted with iron. Such was the force propelling the bolts that they could punch through an enemy's shield and armor and go straight into his flesh; they were unstoppable and proved to be an intimidating and highly effective weapon.

SAPPERS

The sappers were noncombatants, but they were still crucial to the Uruk military machine. They propelled the huge ballistas, carried the bolts and siege ladders, and looked after the two bombs with their precious and deadly cargo as the army marched to Helm's Deep. As the Uruk soldiers attacked, the sappers would have been responsible for raising the ladders and assembling the ballistas for firing. The bow of the ballista was pulled back by twisting a huge rope, and then the fifteen-foot bolt was laid into the breach. The head of the bolt had been designed to fit perfectly into the battlements of Helm's Deep; at its tail was a pulley, through which ran a rope connected to the top of a

siege ladder that lay on the ground. The other end of the rope was held by Uruk sappers, who, once the bolt had been fired into place, ran away from the wall and pulled up the ladder, which was already swarming with dozens of Uruk swordsmen, ready to be delivered directly onto the battlements of the outer keep. Sappers also carried the battering ram from Isengard to the gates of the ancient Rohan refuge, so although they carried no weapon they succeeded in inflicting great damage upon their enemy.

ARMOR

Because Saruman's Orcs were manufacturing a huge amount of armor, and making it as quickly and as efficiently as possible, all of the Uruk-hai were fitted with the same armor. Inevitably, it did not fit as well as the armor of other races, but it served its purpose. Little consideration appears to have been given to the long-term survival of the Uruks, only that they were protected enough to keep them upright and battle-worthy. All of the armor was concentrated on the front, as that was where damage would be most likely: this served to reinforce the attack-only attitude of the Uruks, for if they ever turned their unprotected backs it would mean immediate death. The armor consisted of a leather tunic and groin-guard, over which was worn a short-sleeved mail hauberk (*above right*) and breastplate; the legs were protected with greaves and sabatons (*below*) – these were more for protection when wading through bodies than when in combat, because the knees and thighs were still vulnerable, as were the elbows. The swordsmen (*right*) and pikesmen (*above left*) were additionally fitted with steel vambraces and pauldrons. The only difference in armor is found in the helmets; the basic design for all except the crossbow-men was a bowl shape that was cut around the maw, allowing the Uruk to bite when in close combat; both helmets had a fan-shaped crest and an eye slit, but the swordsmen's was additionally fitted with cheek-plates that extended into blades (*below right*). These were precisely the width of a man's eyes, giving the Uruk an additional, particularly nasty, means of killing his foe. The helmet of the crossbow-men was a type of sallet (*right*), and was fitted with a wide brim that formed the lower edge of the visor.

BERSERKERS

Berserkers were larger, even more fearsome versions of the Uruk-hai, standing about seven feet tall and weighing an estimated three hundred pounds. Before they were sent into battle, it is said, the bowl of their small, tight-fitting helmet was filled with the blood of their enemy, then pushed onto their heads. The intoxicating smell awakened a bloodlust that drove them to a battle-frenzy. Berserkers had no regard for personal safety, wore no armor except their helmets and were expected to fight to the death. Their sole object was to establish a bridgehead; for Helm's Deep they almost certainly would have been trained to climb onto the siege ladders as they were raised up against the Deeping Wall, then to buy enough time for their comrades who were swarming up the ladders and in behind the Berserkers. It proved very difficult to get close enough to wound the Berserkers, so although they numbered only about thirty they were able to inflict heavy losses on the defenders before they were all killed. Berserkers used only one weapon, a huge sword with a five-foot blade and a foot-long double spike at the end; it was a cumbersome sword, requiring an enormous amount of strength to wield it, but the eighteen-inch-long handgrip allowed the Berserker to apply leverage in the swing by placing his hands wide apart. Each side of the four-inch-wide blade was hammered to a sharp edge, and one blow from it could cut a man in half. It was not an elegant or particularly efficient sword – for example, the spikes could get caught in the victim – but the level of intimidation generated by such a nasty weapon was huge.

Helm's Deep battle plan

1. Saruman's army of 10,000 Uruk-hai advances into the valley.
2. The Men of Rohan, a few hundred strong led by King Théoden, crowd the Hornburg, while 200 Elven archers under Aragorn and Haldir line the battlement of the Deeping Wall.
3. The defenders loose volley after volley down upon the Uruk-hai as they close on Helm's Deep. This is answered by a hail of crossbow bolts from the Uruk-hai.
4. Siege ladders are raised against the Deeping Wall, and

Berserkers lead the assault, gaining the battlement and giving the Uruk swordsmen vital time in which to swarm up behind them. Fierce hand-to-hand fighting ensues.

5. Saruman's bombs, placed in a culvert at the foot of the Deeping Wall, are detonated, destroying the middle of the wall along with countless Elves and Uruk-hai.
6. The Uruks send a "tortoise" up the causeway to the Great Gates; through this is carried a battering ram, which is used to break through the gates. Théoden leads the defense of the gates.

7. As Uruk-hai pikesmen pour through the breach in the wall, Elven archers held in reserve fire scores of arrows into them; led by Aragorn, they then charge into the wall of pikes. Superior numbers of Uruk-hai eventually result in the death of all the Elves.

8. The Uruk-hai bring forward giant crossbows that fire grappling hooks into the Outer Court of the Hornburg; these are used to hoist giant siege ladders, perhaps eighty feet tall, which are covered in Uruks, toward the Outer Wall. As they begin to overrun the wall, the defenders retreat into the Hornburg.

9. As the sun begins to rise, Théoden and Aragorn lead the last of the Rohirrim on a charge through the inner and outer courts and down the causeway into the sea of remaining Uruk-hai.

10. At that time, Gandalf appears on the horizon; he and Éomer lead a host of two thousand Rohirrim down a steep scree slope and into the flank of the Uruk-hai.

11. The Uruk-hai, left in disarray by this surprise attack, turn to flee the valley; however, a huge forest of Huorns now covers the entire width of the Deeping Coomb. None escape the forest alive.

Saruman

Saruman the White [TA c.1000 – 3018] was chief and greatest of the Istari, the wizards who came out of the west to aid the Free Peoples in their struggle against Sauron. Saruman was able to exert much control over men's minds, especially through his voice, and was greatly skilled with his hands, earning him the Elven name Curunír, meaning "man of skill." Saruman's vast knowledge of Ring-lore and his researches into the works of Sauron led him to believe that he could use the One Ring to be the ruler of Middle-earth, and he went to Orthanc in TA 2759 specifically to locate and use its palantír to search for it. But in doing so he was soon ensnared by Sauron and became little more than the Dark Lord's puppet, acting out his will. During the latter half of the Third Age his mind turned away from the living things of Middle-earth and toward things of metal and machinery.

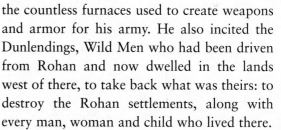

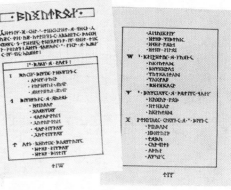

Sauron desired to have a second army that could be used both to destroy Rohan and to form a second pincer with which to crush Gondor, so he instructed Saruman to build him one. Saruman had already recruited the Orcs of the Misty Mountains, but he knew that he would need soldiers who could attack in the daylight. So, by learning from Sauron the foul craft devised by him of combining alchemy and magic, Saruman created his own Uruk-hai. Thousands upon thousands were farmed from the earth. Meanwhile, Saruman used the Orcs to tear down the trees that filled Isengard as fuel for the countless furnaces used to create weapons and armor for his army. He also incited the Dunlendings, Wild Men who had been driven from Rohan and now dwelled in the lands west of there, to take back what was theirs: to destroy the Rohan settlements, along with every man, woman and child who lived there.

The first hundred of Saruman's Uruk-hai were dispatched to intercept the Fellowship and bring any hobbit they found – and thus the Ring – to Isengard; Saruman hoped to seize it before Sauron and claim it for himself. But this would lead to his undoing. Not entirely trusting his Uruk-hai, Saruman also sent a party of

---

ABOVE *Pages recovered from Saruman's study at Orthanc.*
LEFT *Saruman the White was the greatest of his order, but he was brought low by his pride.*

his Orcs, led by Grishnákh, to ensure that the hobbits made it back to Isengard. However, neither group was successful; the hobbits escaped and met with the Ent Treebeard in Fangorn Forest, and showed him the devastation that Saruman had wrought upon the trees of Isengard. In revenge, Treebeard led the Ents in an attack upon Saruman's fortress, flooding its caverns and foundries and trapping

Saruman within Orthanc along with his servant, Gríma Wormtongue.

Realizing that his Uruk raiding party had failed, Saruman had already unleashed the full force of his Uruk army, ten thousand strong, upon the people of Rohan. But when the first people to return to Isengard were Théoden, King of Rohan, Aragorn and Gandalf the White, Saruman knew that all his plans for domination had failed. Scholars still disagree over the fate of the White Wizard. Some maintain that instead of falling at Orthanc under Wormtongue's dagger, he was struck down in the Shire; other theorists suggest that after being humbled he was allowed to leave with his life, and he headed east, taking with him new ideas for an industrialized tyranny that were eagerly embraced by the men of that region.

PALANTÍRI

The Númenóreans, led by Elendil, carried with them to Middle-earth a seedling of the White Tree, Nimloth the Fair, the scepter of Annúminas and the palantíri, seven seeing-stones given them by the Elves. The palantíri were crystal globes, about the size of a man's head, were deepest black in color when not in use. These were distributed throughout Middle-earth in the following manner: Elendil placed one at the tower of Elostirion that looked west over the sea, one at Annúminas and one at the watchtower of Amon Sûl, which sat on Weathertop; Isildur and Anárion took the other four and set them at Orthanc, Minas Anor (Minas Tirith), Osgiliath and Minas Ithil (Minas Morgul). In this way they could communicate across the vast distances that separated the northern and southern kingdoms.

However, by the time of the War of the Ring, only the palantíri of Orthanc and Minas Tirith were still in use, and the stone of Minas Ithil had been taken to Mordor. Once a valuable tool in the war against Sauron, they had now become one of the Dark Lord's chief weapons for gathering information and corrupting the hearts and minds of his foe.

Isengard

URING THE SECOND AGE the Númenóreans were at the height of their power, and built many wondrous and mighty things: the Argonath, towering statues of Isildur and Elendil that guarded the northern boundary of Gondor; the towers and ramparts of the Black Gate; but none more important in the War of the Ring than Isengard.

Inside the ring-wall of Isengard was the tower of Orthanc, which was made from four unbreakable pillars of black stone fused together by means that are still unknown. At the top each was shaped into a horn and in the center of these was a flat platform carved with astronomical symbols.

Orthanc stood five hundred feet high and was surrounded by a deep circular wall a mile in diameter. It housed one of the seven palantíri, so the tower's height would have greatly aided those looking into it, giving them views of a huge area of surrounding land and activity. For this reason Saruman took over the keys of the tower in TA 2759, desiring Isengard both as an impenetrable seat of power and as a means of searching for the One Ring.

There was only one way into the tower: a doorway reached after a climb of thirty-two steps. Inside was the grand chamber, which housed the palantír; off to one side of this was Saruman's study, which contained many arcane artifacts and a library second only to

RIGHT *Isengard was once full of ancient trees and parkland.*
BELOW *The paths of Isengard were laid out in an eight-pointed star.*

Saruman's library contained countless books of arcane lore.

that in Rivendell, the product of nearly three thousand years of research into the lore of Middle-earth. The study window led to a balcony that overlooked the southern half of Saruman's fortress; from here he would have commanded his Uruk army standing in ordered ranks two hundred feet below.

Many and deep were the caverns beneath Isengard, and these were expanded by Saruman's Orcs as he prepared to build an army. Down here were the foundries, the armories, the barracks for the Uruk-hai, and the pits where the ferocious Wargs were penned. Above was desolation and destruction; below was industry and manufacture, where a million creatures were being readied for war.

The one weak spot in Isengard's construction was its dependence upon and proximity to the River Isen. This was exploited by the Ents to devastating effect when they tore down the dam that held back the river, allowing the waters to flood Isengard and wash away the taint that the wizard had brought to the land.

BELOW *A sketch of Orcs maintaining one of Orthanc's great furnaces.*
RIGHT *The waters of the River Isen extinguished Saruman's fires.*

The Rangers of Ithilien

At the time of the War of the Ring, the Rangers were the sole protectors of Gondor's border territories. As their name implies, they ranged the length and breadth of Ithilien, the land that separated the kingdom of Men from the realm of the Dark Lord, Sauron, and were Gondor's scouts as well as its defenders, reporting back to the White City with all significant intelligence. (Unbeknownst to all, Denethor, his mind clouded by grief over the loss of his wife, had begun to use the palantír that had lain unused for centuries in the White Tower. Although this had shown him much of the movement of enemy troops, its use had allowed him to be ensnared by Sauron, who had fed him misinformation that eventually turned his despair into madness.)

Almost since the foundation of the kingdom, Gondor had come under attack from Easterlings in northern Ithilien and Haradrim in the south, so patrols had to be constantly vigilant. Also, because of their relatively few numbers, they – like the Rangers of the north led by Aragorn – relied on skills learned from the Elves: camouflage, stealth and swift attacks of deadly precision. They fought a guerrilla war, using their principal weapon, the

The Rangers' garb was dyed the colors of the woodland: brown, green and gray.

Henneth Annûn was an armory, storehouse and refuge.

was one of many secret refuges set up during the years when Gondor's power was waning, and remained hidden from the enemy during all the years of the War of the Ring; the only outsiders ever to see it and live were Frodo, Sam and Gollum.

As Sauron began mobilizing his armies, it became impossible for the Rangers to continue their patrols and roving attacks, as the enormous numbers of Orcs would have quickly overcome their meager defense, so they withdrew to Osgiliath, crossing the Anduin at their own secret location north of the city or through the sewers that crisscrossed the city. Here, however, it was a different kind of conflict, a slow war of attrition that the Orcs were gradually winning. Eventually the surviving Rangers and soldiers were forced to abandon this last outpost of Gondor and retreat to Minas Tirith, harried all the way by the Nazgûl riding monstrous fell beasts. Many of the Rangers then accompanied Faramir on his doomed ride back to Osgiliath, to try to retake it, but they were cut down in their tracks by hundreds of Orc arrows before they even reached the Rammas Echor. The mortally wounded Faramir was one of the few ever to return.

bow, from within the safety of the trees, harrying their enemies until they were in a state of disarray. If at all possible, they would try to strike the captains first: a leaderless force would often retreat if it lacked self-discipline and control and was too surprised to mount an effective defense. If the enemy numbers were small enough, the Rangers might move in to try to finish them off by sword, although the primary consideration was to preserve the numbers of the Ranger company, as these men were seasoned veterans who would be difficult to replace from the rank and file garrisoned within Minas Tirith. Being a Ranger was considered the most dangerous posting in all of Gondor; their number included only the most loyal and most skillful warriors.

The Rangers had as their base the area known as Henneth Annûn, which consisted of a cave system hidden behind a waterfall that flowed into the Forbidden Pool; it was used as an armory, storehouse and sleeping area. This

WEAPONS

As has been said, the primary weapon of the Rangers was the bow. This was a simple longbow, usually made of a single piece of yew with no adornment or recurving, that stood as much as 80 inches tall when strung. The bows required great strength to draw them fully, and great skill to fire them accurately when holding back the power that they generated: it is estimated that the bows of the Ithilien Rangers had a draw as high as 140 pounds. As there was no arrow-rest, the arrows were fired off the glove. They were made from a variety of woods, as Ithilien was rich in many different types of trees. The arrows averaged about 28 inches in length, with a 4-inch steel broad-headed tip and

green-gold fletches taken from the wild game birds that populated the woods, especially wild turkeys. It is said that a Ranger could consistently hit and kill his target at a range of 200 yards. Although none have ever been found, it is likely that they carried a lighter arrow to be used when hunting small animals, and birds for more feathers. The Rangers carried their arrows in a quiver that was very similar to those used by the Men of Rohan: a leather case with an inner canvas bag that could be drawn up over the arrows to keep them dry, and perhaps also to keep them quiet when they were stalking an enemy. The quiver was strapped tightly to the body rather than worn on the belt like the quivers of the regular Gondorian soldiers. For close work the Rangers carried a standard Gondorian sword that was belted to their hip. [See *Men of Gondor* for a full description.]

FARAMIR

Faramir [TA 2983 – FO 83] was the younger son of Denethor, Ruling Steward of Gondor, and brother to Boromir. While Boromir was very much his father's son, and so was always the favored one, Faramir took after his mother, Finduilas, being more perceptive and deeper thinking than his brother, who preferred solving things with a sword rather than with a word. Yet for all this, the two had great love for each other, and fought side by side during many battles against Sauron's Orcs, most notably in the summer of TA 3018 when Boromir led a successful defense of Osgiliath, even retaking a key position that had been overrun by Orcs. It was following this famous victory that both brothers dreamed of Isildur's Bane, and Boromir decided that he must ride north to try to discover the secret to this riddle. That long and dangerous path would lead him to the answer itself, but it would be his undoing.

Like Boromir, Faramir had his mother's fair hair, yet it must have been some other trait that caused Denethor to turn against his younger son when his wife died. By appointing Faramir captain of the Ithilien Rangers he effectively

Faramir fought alongside his elder brother, Boromir, for the last time in Osgiliath.

Faramir was famed for his skill with a bow.

banished him from the court, and no achievement, however great, would ever win his father's love.

During his time as captain of the Rangers, Faramir became highly skilled in strategic command, yet was also famed for his ability with the bow and sword. He led from the front, and was much respected and loved by his men. He spent many hard years patrolling and fighting running battles in Ithilien, but the advent of Sauron's war upon Gondor led Faramir to withdraw all of his Rangers to Osgiliath: there were not enough of them to mount an effective defense of its eastern border. Faramir led the defense of Osgiliath, fighting bravely to briefly stem the tide of invading Orcs, before overwhelm-

ing numbers forced him to again retreat to Minas Tirith. But under orders from his father, he led a doomed ride to retake the ancient capital city of Gondor. Almost every knight fell before reaching its streets; Faramir once more withdrew the survivors in an attempt to stop the senseless slaughter, but they were preyed upon by Nazgûl that killed all except Faramir, who arrived at the Great Gates mortally wounded.

In the last throes of his madness, Denethor tried to burn his still-living son on a funeral pyre but was thwarted by Gandalf and Pippin. Faramir was eventually healed by Aragorn, and found new life and love in the arms of Éowyn, niece of Théoden. He was appointed Steward of Gondor under King Elessar and Prince of Ithilien, where he lived with his new bride in happiness.

Faramir dressed in the same garb as his men, save that his leather tunic bore the Tree of Gondor in silver, indicating his exalted position within the Gondorian army.

RIGHT *Faramir's unique sword and helmet signified his position within the Gondorian army.*
BELOW *Two hundred knights rode to their doom on the Pelennor Fields; only one returned.*

Bows of Middle-earth

THE BOW WAS THE FIRST SOPHISTICATED WEAPON to take attack beyond the range of a warrior's normal physical capabilities. Its primary use, however, was for hunting, where, by taking the hunter outside the area of an animal's range of perception, it allowed him to bring down the beast before it had got wind of him. On the battlefield, it would prove invaluable in allowing a warrior to strike at his foes before they could become a threat to him – the side that possessed superior archery nearly always triumphed in battle, as it could reduce the enemy force and thus, hopefully, have superior numbers when the battle moved to the stage of close combat.

Bows were principally made of wood, and yew, ash and mallorn are all recorded as being used, the last exclusive to the Elves of Lothlórien (*left*) as this was the only place in Middle-earth where the legendary tree of Númenor would grow. (Living mallorn wood probably could not have been harvested without the observance of lengthy ritual and many offerings to Yavanna.) The bows of the ancient Númenóreans, however, are said to have been made of hollow steel, a feat achievable only by the famed Guild of Weaponsmiths.

A longbow was usually made from a single piece of wood: to start with, the stave that was cut from the tree needed to be about twice the length of the draw, plus a fifth, and at least three inches thick. With a small axe or knife the bark was cut away until the back of the stave had been reduced to one continuous growth ring. The tips of the stave would then have been sealed before seasoning the wood, allowing it to dry until all moisture was gone, a process that could take months or just weeks, depending on the process used and the

The Wood-elves of Lórien would have limbered up to prepare for the long battle.

urgency to produce the bow. If a heavy draw was required, the stave would be reduced until it consisted entirely of heartwood, or the middle growth ring of the tree. If a handle was desired, the middle of the stave was marked with a four or five-inch length, together with another couple of inches extending into the upper and lower limbs, in which the handle would flare out to the full width of the stave. This middle section would be the unbending part of the bow; the rest of the limbs would then be cut back with axe, knife and coarse grit to give the stave flexibility. All the while this was being done, the bow would be continually tested and flexed, introducing a curve into the fibers of the wood while assessing the draw weight of the bow. It was crucial to make sure there were no flat spots in the curve of the limbs and that they bent evenly from the fades to the nocks. The bow was then nocked, strung and tested, with the draw weight kept slightly above what was required to allow for finishing, sealing and other decoration.

A shortbow was constructed of a composite of materials and was sometimes curved away from the final direction in order to get an increased amount of power from it: this was called a recurve bow, and some of them were so strong that they almost formed a circle before being strung. When the limbs were pulled back they were under extremely high tension, even before the bow was drawn: it was a way of taking a short bow and getting a huge amount of power from it. Typically, the middle of a composite bow would be a thin wooden slat, which would be strengthened with a harder wood or horn on the impressive

side – the side that faced the archer as he fired – and sinew on the side that was under tension as he drew the bow. All of these elements would be held together with animal-based glues and bindings. An Orc bow would follow this basic principle but only in the crudest way: horn would be used to reinforce the ends of the bow, and the whole construction would be bound using whatever materials came to hand, regardless of their suitability or longevity. Some lurid firsthand accounts of Orc battles describe bows that were bound with strips of skin that had been torn from their victims while still fresh. Such a bow, made without any understanding of design or method, would have been vastly inferior to those employed by the more advanced cultures.

When traveling over long distances, a warrior would customarily carry the bow unstrung, either holding the stave in his hand or slung across his back and strapped to the quiver. If the bow was kept strung for long periods, both the stave and the string would lose some of their tension, making the weapon less effective. Of course, if the terrain was likely to harbor either enemies or quarry the bow would be carried strung. In wet weather, the string would be carried in a pouch to keep it dry, or even under the helmet, and would already have loops at its ends; in this way the bow could be restrung in a matter of a moments.

Because a bow was held under great tension, it required great upper-body strength to use one

TOP LEFT *The middle of the Gondorian longbow was thicker than the limbs, providing a rigid stave.*
TOP RIGHT *The Elven bow featured delicate carvings that were painted gold.*
RIGHT *The bow of the Moria Orcs was a composite of metal, horn and sinew.*

Bows were often strapped to the quiver for traveling. The superior quality of Lórien string allowed Legolas to carry his bow strung.

with any accuracy or consistency. Each bow has a "draw weight": this is the amount of force, measured in pounds, required to draw the string back to its optimum position, which is usually the distance from the hand holding the bow to the bowman's eyetooth. For a bow with a draw of 150 pounds, drawing the string fully back would equate to hanging a weight of 150 pounds from the bow to reach the same distance. That would be almost like lifting a fully grown man with one arm, with all of the weight concentrated in the two or three fingers that were hooked around the string; it is little wonder that all but the most hardy bowmen wore leather gloves on their draw-hand! To control this power, the bowman would draw the string, hold it for a beat or two to steady his aim, then release; if he held it any longer his hand would begin to shake, and even a minor wobble would mean a deviation of many yards. It is likely that every bowman trained for long years, advancing from target shooting to hunting and then on to combat as his ability increased, so any bowman seen on the battlefield would have been at the very peak of his skills, and would have been crucial to the success of the armies of the Free Peoples.

Gondorian longbows are said to have had a draw weight of at least 140 pounds.

144

Gondor

WHEN THE DÚNEDAIN FAITHFUL FLED to Middle-earth after the sinking of Númenor, their great ships landed at ports such as Pelargir, which had been established long ago in the Second Age. From here they sailed up the Anduin, eventually founding the kingdom of Gondor in the lands surrounding the White Mountains. It was important for these "Ship-kings" to have close access to the sea, so their cities were all built within easy reach of the River Anduin. Greatest of these was Osgiliath, which lay on both sides of the river, with each half connected by a wide stone bridge; here was housed the chief of the four palantíri of the south kingdom. West of Osgiliath was Minas Anor, its massive battlements built from the mountain to which it was adjoined. To the east, in the shadow of the Mountains of Mordor, was built Minas Ithil; when

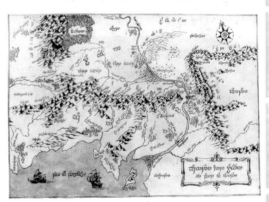

Gondor was founded in SA 3320 it was believed that Sauron had perished beneath the waves, so there was no reservation about settling so close to his realm. Yet this nearly proved the Dúnedain's undoing when Sauron launched a sudden attack upon the unwary population. Minas Ithil was lost to Sauron's Orcs and became the haunt of the Nazgûl, and it was only a desperate defense of Osgiliath's eastern side that prevented the loss of Gondor's capital city.

ABOVE *A second-Age Elven map of Gondor. The Númenórean ships reflect Gondor's active trading with the Elves.*
LEFT *Osgiliath and the River Anduin seen from the northwest.*
BELOW *The Ered Nimrais, or White Mountains, which ran west from Minas Tirith almost to the sea.*

Views of Minas Morgul and of Osgiliath, with the dome of the palantír visible in the middle of the River Anduin.

However, it was from within that Gondor began to fail: in the early fifteenth century of the Third Age the so-called Kin-strife began, a civil war sparked by the diminishing of the royal Númenórean bloodline. Growing friction between the two factions eventually erupted into mass bloodshed, with many in the invincible Gondorian navy taking the side of the usurper, eventually fleeing Pelargir to found an independent lordship in Umbar; ever after, they would be a menace to Gondor, and from their number would come the dreaded Corsairs. The civil war was costly in terms of loss of population and loss of reputation. The once-subdued nations of the Easterlings and Haradrim began ever-bolder attacks upon Gondor's southern and eastern borders, while the dissident navy harried its coastline. Then, two hundred years later, a great plague swept out of the east: this proved catastrophic for Osgiliath; nearly all of its people died, and those who didn't fled, spreading the disease to the rest of Middle-earth. Osgiliath was left to decay and Gondor declined, its much-reduced population now concentrated inside Minas Anor, renamed Minas Tirith, the city of guard, watching their enemies steadily encroach upon the once-great kingdom.

The Great Gates of Minas Tirith.

MINAS TIRITH

Minas Tirith (meaning "Tower of Guard") was built on the outthrust shoulder of Mount Mindolluin, the easternmost peak in the chain of the White Mountains. When building this great city, the Dúnedain would have mined the mountains for countless tons of the white stone and marble contained within them. Originally named Minas Anor after Isildur's brother Anárion, the city's name was changed after the fall of Minas Ithil to Sauron's Nazgûl in TA 2002. It stood on seven walled levels: each wall had only one gate and each was situated in a different part of the wall. The Great Gates of oak and iron faced east toward Mordor. Because of its shape, the southern half of the city was in shade most of the time and so was considered the less desirable part to live in; all of the wealthier people lived in the north-facing half. The height of the city, from the foot of the gates to the top of the Tower of Ecthelion, was estimated to be a

Trebuchets were mounted along the battlements of the lower levels.

thousand feet or more, and the diameter of the city almost three-quarters of a mile. But the most remarkable feature was the spectacular towering bastion of stone, shaped like the keel of a ship, that rose from behind the gates up to the level of the citadel on the seventh tier, a quarter of a mile above. It gave an unparalleled view of the city and the Pelennor Fields, all the way to Osgiliath and the River Anduin, five miles away, as it flowed around the edge of the fields, and the Mountains of Mordor beyond looming on the horizon.

The outer wall had a wide, battlemented parapet that was further strengthened by towers along its perimeter. Each of the outer wall's towers was armed with a trebuchet that could launch boulders down upon any attackers, as were many on the second, third and even fourth levels, creating a battery one hundred strong. The combination of the weight of the missile, the force of the trebuchet's swing and gravity would have made a devastating impact, particularly when launched from the upper levels. Although the trebuchets were rarely used before the War of the Ring, the crews assigned to them would have tested and maintained their working effectiveness, and hauled up and replenished the supply of boulders.

The White City had never been breached until the Siege of Gondor, when its Great Gates were finally broken by the giant battering ram, Grond, wielded by Mountain Trolls, and its battlements were overrun by Orcs pouring out of siege towers. For the first time Minas Tirith's defenders were forced to fight within their beloved city's walls, even firing down upon the lower levels with trebuchets from above. Yet this would be the last time that the gates were breached, for after the War of the Ring a company of Dwarves led by Gimli repaired them, using precious supplies of mithril to make them truly unassailable.

The White City commanded views all the way to Mordor and beyond.

The Men of Gondor

GONDOR HAD FALLEN INTO DECLINE during the latter half of the Third Age, reduced from an empire covering almost a third of western Middle-earth to practically a city-state. Once they were conquerors of all they surveyed, and now they were living largely within the confines of Minas Tirith.

Much of Gondor's problem was that her people had lacked effective leadership for generations. Gone were the kings of old, embodying her strength and grandeur. Instead, Gondor's ruling stewards had looked only to maintaining the status quo, trying to preserve the glory of what once was without inspiring the people who looked to them for direction. Initially this was born of humility, not wanting to change what they did not feel it was their right to change, but gradually, as their sense of self-importance grew, they ruled in the name of past glories but lacked the appetite or vision to lead Gondor to new ones. However, the people of Gondor seemed oblivious to the decline that was happening around them, and still saw themselves as superior to the other mannish cultures in Middle-earth.

BELOW *Osgiliath was the last outpost manned by Gondor.*
RIGHT *Regular parades and drills ensured military discipline.*

Although it had an infantry-based army, Gondor still maintained a small cavalry.

The Men of Gondor had changed from the times of the "ship-kings": they were shorter and stockier than their ancestors, standing between five foot eight inches and six feet, but some still sported the short beards popular in ancient Númenor. They wore their dark curly hair long, and the warm climate of the south kingdom gave them an olive complexion. They were a proud culture, with great respect for a heritage that had instilled in them a love of arts and learning, and they developed a code of honor. In battle they employed strategies that had been drilled into them at their military academy; they marched in controlled, ordered ranks, deeply aware of the hierarchical structure of the division or company in which they fought. The Gondorians' size meant that they were strong but slow, so this would naturally have led them to favor wearing heavy armor, as they had little natural agility with which to avoid enemy blows. Their strength was their greatest weapon, and it led them to favor close combat, trading blows with their enemy by hacking and slashing, and smashing them with their heavy shields.

Yet the military machinery was still maintained within the city, and people were still fiercely proud of their heritage and their city. It is probable that every man of Gondor trained in a military academy after finishing his schooling, then found another profession or became a full-time soldier. Therefore, despite the weaknesses introduced through the ineffective rule of the stewards, the people of Minas Tirith were still ready and willing to defend themselves against the might of Mordor as the shadow stretched out, eager to cover the White City in darkness.

LONGBOW

The Gondorian army contained specific divisions of longbowmen, who carried just this weapon. On the battlefield they would form the rearmost ranks, and would fire volley after volley into the air so that the arrows would come crashing down upon the heads of the enemy; an experienced archer could send up to five arrows into the air before the first hit its target. This devastating assault always formed the first stage in a Gondorian attack, as it would greatly demoralize and weaken the enemy. When defending the city, these longbowmen would have been lined up along the battlements of the lower levels and would have kept up a rain of arrows upon the besiegers, using

their superior elevation to outshoot the enemy. The Gondorian longbow was deceptively simple in appearance, a plain stave of heartwood, about sixty-eight inches tall and stained dark brown, slightly thicker around the handgrip with little tapering, but generations of craftsmanship were behind each one. The bow was capable of sending an arrow 200 yards with consistent accuracy. The long black arrows averaged about twenty-eight inches in length, with a four-inch steel broad-head tip and blue-gray fletches taken from the abundant numbers of gulls and other seabirds that followed the Anduin – and its fishing boats – upriver. Because of the bows' length, the longbowmen wore their quiver hung from a suspension system on their left hip and drew the arrow like a sword.

SWORD

Minas Tirith was well supplied with blacksmiths, all manufacturing weapons and armor for the state army to a uniform standard of size and shape. They all featured the same motif, of a seven-tiered city, somewhere upon them. For the swords, the motif appeared on the bronze pommel, its considerable size serving to counterbalance the wide unfullered blade, milled to a diamond-shaped cross-section, that measured about twenty-eight inches in length; the crescent-shaped guard was also made of bronze. The size and weight of the one-handed weapon were ideally suited to the hacking and slashing method of attack used by the Gondorians. The plain wooden scabbard was covered in dark-stained leather and fitted with a bronze locket: the bronze Minas Tirith motif appeared just below this within curving lines of bronze, perhaps representing the Rammas Echor and River Anduin.

SPEAR

An eight-foot ash spear was sometimes carried as a secondary weapon by the Gondorian soldiers, to be used as a defensive wall against enemy charges. It was not designed to be thrown; rather it was for stabbing and withdrawing. Its leaf-shaped steel blade would open a large wound yet could be pulled out with ease. Unlike the spears of the Fountain Guard, it featured no guard behind the blade so there was nothing for an opponent to grab on to. The motif appeared in steel at the base of the blade.

ARMOR

Since the earliest days of their kingdom, the Men of Gondor had always had access to a rich supply of iron ore and so had been able to produce large amounts of steel weaponry and armor. They also would have greatly benefited from their Dúnedain ancestors' contact with the Elves, so their smiths would have been the most gifted of all the mannish races. They would have delighted in exploiting their double good-fortune in their armor. Yet for all their technological advancement, they still harked back to the glory days of old Númenor, so there was a level of detail and romanticism that comes with any culture that once was greater than it is now. There appears to have been a need to include so much prestige in what they did then because they lived in the shadow of what had gone before, which is why their armor featured gold trim; it was a way of asserting to themselves and to others their status and prestige.

Armor did not require the same quality of ore as did swords – it had a low-to-medium carbon content, but it could still be heat-treated, or tempered, like a sword blade, making it stronger. It was a special skill of the smiths in those days to know the ore they were working with, how best to treat it, and whether the steel it made would be best for arms or armor. During the three thousand years of the Third Age they had succeeded in refining the type of armor, so that instead of the heavier mail hauberks worn at the Last Alliance, they were now protected with steel plate armor; this was "alwite" armor, meaning that it was not faced, or covered, with any material, unlike, say, the armor worn by the royal court at Edoras. The blacksmith's level of skill meant that he could

151

produce plate armor that was lighter yet stronger, almost to the point that a one-handed sword would be ineffective against it. (However, an axe or mace, or other sharp-pointed weapon, could still smash or cut through it, causing fatal damage.)

All Gondorian soldiers were kitted out in the same unified armor design: a woolen undertunic and hose, whose sleeves and legs, from the knees down, were of mail, attached with leather points; the tunic and hose were interlinked by a small leather belt that ran through leather loops extending from both items. A short, sleeveless woolen tunic was worn over this, which served as an aketon. A steel two-piece collar was put on next, each half of which had a raised flange to protect the neck. Next the steel cuirass, embossed with the Tree of Gondor, was placed over the head and tightened with leather straps; it is probable that in the interests of speed, one half of the cuirass would have already been tightened and the five-lamed pauldrons already strapped on to the shoulder area of the cuirass, thus requiring them only to be strapped around the arms to secure them; the lower lame was also embossed with a branch of the tree. Each pauldron was flanged to protect the side of the neck. The breastplate flared out at the base so that any blows down to the stomach or groin would be deflected away from the body; it also served as a handy anchor from which to hang the sword or quiver belt. Below the cuirass hung a pair of curved, six-lamed tassets that were also strapped to the cuirass, offering upper leg protection. The intention with steel plate armor was always to try to deflect the blow; for that reason most surfaces were smooth and curved, so that the weapon would slide off. Lastly, steel greaves and vambraces were strapped on, leather gloves were pulled on and the barbut-style helmet was donned. Although mail covered the soldier's arms, and he carried a shield, he was further protected by the vambrace, which extended around and over the elbow. All of this preparation was done in the barracks; once armored, they passed through the armory to be given their swords, spears and shields, then mustered outside in ranks, ready to march to war. It is worth noting that a Gondorian soldier's legs were encumbered with armor only from the knees down: like any infantry, they would be expected to march great distances, then fight. Every step taken, accelerating, then stopping, when wearing metal armor would have been extremely tiring, so infantry would have had relatively little protection on their legs and would be heavily protected from the hips up.

SHIELD

Although outwardly similar, the Third Age Gondorian shield differed in various ways from that carried by their ancestors at the Last Alliance; the most significant change was that the bottom edge was straight rather than extending down into a curved point. This can be explained by the diminished height of the warriors. The tall Dúnedain who marched into Mordor had fallen in great numbers, plague had killed many more, and the bloodline of Númenor had been almost lost among the women of ordinary birth who now represented the majority of the female population. Therefore, the Gondorian warrior was closer in stature to the Men of Middle-earth than of Númenor, so this obviated the need for such a long shield. The shield was constructed the same way it had been for thousands of years, with thin planks of wood built up in overlapping layers, but it was now also fitted with a covering of leather that had been glued and pinned to the wood. It was still reinforced with metal strips along its top and bottom edges, but the metal Tree of Gondor device was now merely painted on. A further deviation was observable in the device itself: during the long years of the rule of stewards, Gondor no longer included the royal emblems of the crown and seven stars on its armor or its banners: a small but significant indication of the way in which the ruling stewards viewed their "kingdom." There was no change in the design and location of the handgrip and enarme, whose diagonal positioning allowed the shield to be held flat to the forearm so that it could be used to push enemy blows up and away from the body, allowing the soldier to follow through with his own attack to his opponent's now-unprotected body.

Denethor

DENETHOR [TA c.2935 – 3019] WAS THE LAST of the ruling stewards of Gondor, his badges of office being a hexagonal silver ring set with obsidian and marked with a gold star and a white scepter with a gold capital. Like most of his predecessors, Denethor did not look with favor upon an heir of Isildur returning to sit on the throne of Gondor, and he was therefore wary of Aragorn, son of Arathorn, last of the line of kings: he felt particularly threatened by Aragorn's appearance during the times of upheaval that preceded the War of the Ring. In his youth, Denethor had suspected that the "Thorongil" who had served under his father, Ecthelion II, and who had commanded great loyalty and respect among his father's troops, was in fact Aragorn, and that Gandalf was already at work sowing the seeds for the return of the rightful king of Gondor. In this he was not mistaken, and throughout his life Denethor was always deeply mistrustful of Gandalf and his protégé.

The ruling steward sat beneath the royal throne, which in turn was overshadowed by a great bronze crown.

154

Denethor constantly wore a full-mail hauberk to ward off indolence.

As ruling steward, Denethor had access to one of the three surviving palantíri; the seeing-stone was housed in the White Tower of Ecthelion that stood at the very summit of Minas Tirith. In times past this had been used by the kings and stewards to keep watch over the realm of Gondor by communicating with the seeing-stones at Orthanc, Osgiliath and Minas Ithil. But Sauron's forces had overrun Minas Ithil, the traitorous Saruman had taken charge of Orthanc and Osgiliath's stone had been lost, so the stone of Minas Tirith had not been used for generations. During the War of the Ring Denethor, grown grim after the death of his wife, ill-advisedly chose to use it to try to counter Sauron's moves, and, like Saruman, he was ensnared by Sauron. Despite having a strong will and keen intelligence, Denethor was gradually driven into despair and madness by Sauron's manipulation of what he saw in the stone, and eventually immolated himself on a pyre he had lit for himself and his younger son, Faramir.

SWORD

Although Denethor had ceased active service in the Gondorian army once he became steward, he still carried a ceremonial sword. Standing about four feet in length, it was two-handed, with a wide blade that had been fullered to reduce its weight. The heavily etched bronze guard was in a crescent shape, rather than the traditional cross seen on all swords of Númenórean ancestry, and the long hand-grip was swaged with ten bronze rings and covered in finest leather. The bronze pommel had an unusual half-moon shape and was also heavily etched with symbols and scrollwork. The leather scabbard matched the sword in workmanship, and featured numerous bronze plates that had been fixed to it, probably by successive stewards, some in the shape of the Tree of Gondor, others etched with stylized designs and other scroll-work. In all, it was a kingly weapon for the man who wielded power from a seat beneath the throne of Gondor.

Boromir

Boromir [TA 2978 – 3019], son of Denethor, was a prince of Gondor in all but name: he was the scion of a noble house and heir apparent to a ruling tradition that stretched back for a thousand years. He was great in stature, tall and broad, and for many in the White City of Minas Tirith it was as if one of their revered Númenórean ancestors walked among them once more. Elder brother to Faramir, Boromir was the favored son and in many ways aligned himself with his father, the ruling steward; yet there was still great love between the two brothers. Although flawed in character, Boromir had honor and nobility; he was a man who believed passionately in the greatness of his kingdom and would have defended its people to the very end.

Boromir was tall and strong, and one of the most skilled warriors in all of Gondor with a sword. His stamina and physical strength, together with a forceful and commanding personality, meant that he had quickly risen through the ranks of the military academy. His fellow soldiers of Gondor saw him as a true leader and were willing to follow him anywhere. One of Boromir's most famous successes as a captain in the Gondorian army occurred when, accompanied by Faramir, he led a division into Osgiliath and repelled a horde of Orcs that had overrun the former capital city, driving them back across the bridge into the eastern half. Boromir personally slew

ABOVE *Boromir was one of Gondor's greatest captains.*
RIGHT *The Horn of Gondor, traditionally carried by the heir to the throne.*

many of the orcs, including the captain. This victory gave the Men of Gondor a vital breathing space and allowed them to bring in reinforcements to strengthen and secure their hard-won outpost. It was Boromir's finest hour.

Following a powerful dream shared by both brothers, in which they learned that Isildur's Bane had been found, a reluctant Boromir was commanded by his father to ride north as the ambassador for Gondor to attend the Council of Elrond. Although he argued that the One Ring could be used as a weapon against Sauron, Boromir eventually bowed to the will of the council and agreed to join the Fellowship on its quest to destroy the Ring in Mordor. It will never be known whether Boromir intended from the beginning to take the Ring to Gondor, or if the influence of the Ring itself corrupted him, but he tried to take it from Frodo and this led to his doom at the hands of Saruman's Uruk-hai. A warrior to the end, Boromir left a heap of Uruk corpses around him while single-handedly defending the two hobbits, Merry and Pippin, before eventually falling under a rain of huge black arrows. He was given a hero's funeral by Aragorn, Legolas and Gimli, who recognized in him a man who would have been worthy to be called king.

SWORD

Boromir's sword was like its owner: big, broad and powerful. To use it single-handed required someone with great strength in his arm and wrist, both of which this skilled warrior had in abundance. The blade was over three inches across at its widest point; it had a flattened diamond shape in section with an equally wide fuller in order to keep the weight down. However, the fuller ended some way short of the tip, thereby keeping as much strength in the end of the blade as possible. It was sharpened on both edges and tapered acutely at the tip, which meant that it would have been equally effectively for slashing against lightly armored opponents and for thrusting into more heavily protected foe. The guard showed a warrior's flourish in that it was formed from a square-edged piece of steel that had been twisted before being curved into a crescent. The guard was the same shape as that on his father's sword, as well as those on all Third Age Gondorian swords. The handgrip was wide like the blade, matched to Boromir's hand, and the pommel was an elegant and simple piece of steel, again large to counterbalance the weight of this warrior's blade. The scabbard was wood covered in leather that had been decorated with crisscrossing strips of leather down its length together with a steel locket and an elegant steel chape that matched the shape of the pommel. It was attached directly to the belt so that it hung straight down; the belt was a beautifully worked piece of leather that had been stamped with a delicate leaf pattern repeated along its length. It may be that this was a gift from his mother. Boromir also carried a dagger that was little brother to the sword, matching its blade shape and pommel design; the only difference was that it was enhanced with bronze details; the handgrip was wrapped in fine bronze wire instead of leather, the pommel was gilded with bronze and the guard was formed of a single piece of shaped bronze. Unusually for a dagger, the wide blade was fullered so that in all respects it resembled the tip of Boromir's sword.

SHIELD

Like his sword, the shield that Boromir carried was of a singular design, so it would have been easily recognizable to his men when in combat. Its circular shape and simple design were reminiscent of a buckler, although it would have been too large to be worn on the arm when fighting two-handed. The wood frame had been dyed black, and in its center was a large steel boss that was riveted to the back of the shield; fixed into the boss was a handle made of horn that was edged with bronze rings. Around the edge were engraved the wings and seven stars of Gondor's noble heritage. When not using it, Boromir would have carried his shield over his shoulder by using the finely tooled leather guige that was riveted to the boss and to the steel rim that ran around the edge of the shield, again secured by a number of rivets.

It was a solid piece of work that could have been wielded quickly and effectively; the curved, circular shield had no points that an enemy could catch on, so their blows would slide across and past the shield. When this happened, the attacker's forward momentum would unbalance him, allowing Boromir to bring his sword down upon his outthrust and exposed arm and neck. Whereas if the blow was light enough, the upraised shield would arrest the swing of the blow and Boromir could thrust his sword under his foe's shield and into his belly.

ARMOR

Boromir would have had access to a variety of armor in Minas Tirith, but would probably have favored the plate and mail of the typical Gondorian soldier when engaged in close combat on the field of battle. This would have suited his size: being a big man with a big sword, he would have worn an appropriate level of protection. There would be little point in carrying a heavy sword and shield into battle if he was only lightly armored in leather; conversely, if he had gone to the trouble of putting on what was effectively two sets of armor he would have wanted to wield a weapon that could inflict significant damage while he was so encumbered. (See *Men of Gondor* for a description of this type of armor.)

When Boromir embarked on his long journey to Rivendell, he would have wanted to protect himself but would have been conscious of not tiring his horse; it would be more useful to have speed at his disposal so that he could escape an attack rather than stand and face it and, in all likelihood, lose his mount in the process. So, his armor for the journey would have been a combination of traveling clothes and steel protection that was functional and comfortable.

Boromir's leggings were of a soft dark velvet, almost black in color, which tied at the waist by means of a drawstring; tall leather boots were worn over these. His tunic was of soft burgundy wool, to which had been fixed a collar and upper sleeves made of thick leather. The arm from the elbow down to the wrist was protected by mail that had been stitched to these sleeves using leather points; to prevent them chafing, they were lined with quilted soft gray silk that had been patterned with the stars of Gondor. The tunic was open at the front although it could be laced up with rawhide points. Over this was worn a red silk robe that came down to the elbow and shin; the sleeves were heavily embroidered with gold wire in the pattern of stars, and a similarly embroidered black velvet collar completed this sumptuous item. The robe was split to the groin and open to the chest to allow it to be worn while riding and to be easily removed; the opening was secured with metal catches. Over the robe went a black leather sleeveless robe, of the same weight as his sleeves, which also went down to the shins. Because of the heavy sword and shield that Boromir carried, he would not have needed or wanted to further encumber his arms. Both forearms were merely protected with two-piece leather vambraces – an inner patterned guard and an outer plate of boiled leather tooled with the Tree of Gondor device, then worked in silver – which were strapped around the wrists; ordinarily these would have been steel but the mail sleeves precluded the need for this. The arm protection was completed by a pair of leather gauntlets. The last item worn by Boromir on his travels was a beautifully made cloak of heavily embroidered burgundy velvet edged in fur and with two steel clasps: a princely item that would have left no one in any doubt as to his importance within the Gondorian culture.

159

The Fountain and Citadel Guards

Although part of the military structure of Gondor, these ceremonial guards were probably hand-picked from the elite in the training academies, as their role was more vocation than duty. For unlike their comrades in the infantry and cavalry, they had but one task: to protect the sacred White Tree that stood in the Court of the Fountain, and to guard the citadel and the ruling steward. The Fountain Guards were forbidden to speak when on duty, and wore silk masks as a reminder to all visitors as well as the guards themselves. The traditional title of captain-general of the guard was given to the heir of the ruling steward: at the time of the War of the Ring this would have been Boromir, but the title was apparently conferred on Faramir only after the death of his father, by King Elessar. The Fountain Guards saw no action during the Siege of Gondor, and likely would have remained at their post even if Minas Tirith burned all around them.

WEAPONS

The Fountain Guards carried ten-foot-long ash spears as their primary weapon; presumably the intention was to use this to keep any who might try from reaching the White Tree. The spear featured a unique crescent-shaped guard bearing the Minas Tirith device at its center, which extended into a one-foot-long ridged blade. On their belt they carried a sword that differed in only one way from the standard Gondorian sword: on its pommel was engraved the Tree of Gondor device instead of the Minas Tirith icon. The Fountain Guards carried no shield, perhaps as an indication that if they failed in their duty their life was forfeit. The Citadel Guards carried the weapons of the regular soldier – sword and spear – but like the Fountain Guards they had no shield.

ARMOR

The Citadel Guards wore the same outfit as ordinary Gondorian soldiers, but this was enhanced with a gold-edged black tunic worn under the cuirass and a black cloak with gold embroidery; these would have indicated to all their elevated position within the military structure, as would their helmet, which featured a bronze star device on their noseguard and the brass wings that had been riveted on the sides.

The armor of the Fountain Guards reflected their ceremonial status and their ancient lineage stretching back to the kings of Númenor themselves. Over a long black robe was worn a full-length mail hauberk, which in turn was covered with a white linen sleeveless robe that had been embroidered in different colored threads with beautiful Númenórean patterning. Unique among the Gondorian soldiery, the guards' cuirass was embellished with the seven stars and crown in brass over the tree device; this was because their loyalty was first to Elendil's lost house before the ruling sword. A steel collar, worn under the cuirass, protected the throat. A rich black woolen cloak, embroidered in gold with the same pattern as the robe, was tied around the shoulders, and over this was worn large, five-lamed pauldrons that swept around the shoulders like silver wings; the central and largest lame was embossed with a stylized curving branch, clearly a continuation of the Tree device on the cuirass; a stop-rib was riveted to the pauldron, to protect the guard's neck from a sideswipe. Last, but most important, was the great Númenórean sea-helm: it shone with such a brilliance that it was rumored to be made entirely of mithril, although none now survive to verify this amazing claim. From diagrams discovered in the city's archives, it can be seen that these helmets were similar in shape to the barbuts worn by the regular soldiers, but were adorned with brass patterning around the cheek and nose-guard areas. The most striking feature, however, was the crest, which extended out from the sides of the helm in two foot-long plumes of purest white gull feathers, giving the impression of a winged crown. To any visitor to the Citadel they would have appeared as a vision, a tantalizing glimpse of the glory of Númenor, of a distant past now lost beneath the waves.

161

Orcs of Mordor

SAURON WOULD HAVE LEARNED MUCH from his defeat at the end of the Second Age. He realized that his Orcs had lacked the discipline and military mind to be able to fight the well-trained and organized armies of Elves and Men, and had lost so much because they had been outthought as well as outfought. During the Third Age the Dark Lord had clearly introduced a more regimented structure into his army of Orcs, their captains training them to march and even fight in formation. They were also trained to do specific tasks; among the vast horde that marched out of Mordor there were sappers and engineers, to help work the catapults and build and repair bridges so that the army could cross the River Anduin without being slowed by Osgiliath's single dilapidated bridge. Where the Orcs faced by the Last Alliance were an undisciplined rabble, little more than animals driven by bloodlust rather than common sense, those that marched on the White City marched with a purpose, understanding

BELOW *Orcs of the Third Age were much more disciplined than their forebears.*

– albeit on a simplistic level – military strategy and how to coordinate an attack for maximum effect. There was also more thought behind their method of attack: they still used the whirling, hacking style when striking with a sword, but this was accompanied by more of a sense of self-preservation, and the shield was used defensively, not just as another implement with which to club at their enemy. In all, the Orcs that poured out of Mordor were almost a match for the Uruk-hai that had been created to supplant them, and if not for the Army of the Dead they would have succeeded in overrunning the Free Peoples of Middle-earth.

WEAPONS

So many different types of weapons were recovered from the Pelennor Fields that it is almost impossible to say if there was a preferred weapon among the Orcs. These creatures probably would have reached for whatever was nearest to hand when going into battle, seizing anything that they thought would get the job done. Also, as they were considered totally expendable, they would not have received any training in the use of a specific weapon. Most likely the weapon would be created out of whatever materials were on hand and in whatever shape best suited the crudely fashioned iron pieces that came out of their furnaces. Wood was certainly scarce in western Mordor and would have needed to be scavenged from the more fertile lands of Ithilien and Lithlad, that part of Mordor in which were found the slave-fields that provided food and other materials for Sauron's army. One likely consideration, however, would have been to increase their weapons' reach, which ordinarily would have been inferior to those of their enemy.

Therefore, many staff weapons (or crude approximations of them), such as spears, halberds, gisarmes and pikes, were carried. These were three to six feet long and could also be used against cavalry.

An important weapon for the besieging Orcs would have been the bow, as this would have been the only way of assaulting the defenders prior to the breaching of the Great Gates. The bows carried by the Orcs were short composite bows, made mostly from horn and strung with sinew. As Orcs did not ride, they would have made something that could be easily carried on their back, keeping their hands free. Their lack of skill or craft would have limited the effectiveness of the bows, however, with only those in the front ranks likely to have had the range to trouble the Gondorians.

Like most cultures, the Orcs would have favored the sword for close combat; although the axe required less metal and was easier to make, the sword had a longer cutting edge and was a faster attacking weapon. If their sword was more finely worked, it is probable that it had been traded for with their allies the Easterlings, in the case of scimitars, or picked up on the battlefield if a straight-bladed weapon. That said, the Orcs did have the ability to fashion their own swords and, though crude, they would have been brutally effective.

ARMOR

Orc armor was as varied as their weaponry, seemingly with no two outfits the same. Although there is a view that there was no organized manufacturing of armor or weapons in Mordor, that each Orc had to protect and arm itself, it is likely that there were isolated foundries, leading to some uniformity within groups. However, armor was to some extent a reflection of each individual Orc: one might protect its chest with plate whereas another would not want to be encumbered in this way. The only consistency appears to have been the need to cover as much of the body as pos-

sible, in order to block out the hated sun. They would cover their heads with helmets fitted with visors if available, or with rags if not. Helmets were another area in which the personality of the Orc would be apparent: some were full-faced helms, some had trap-door visors, while others had beaklike nasals to protect the face.

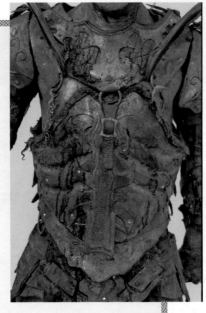

Any material would have been used, regardless of its condition, for Orcs were indifferent to the filth and stench of the corpse-rags and rotting hide that covered them.

Their metal-working capability extended from hammering out sheets of cast iron, roughly cutting them and strapping them on with hide or twine to producing mail of crude effectiveness. Many Orcs also managed to gather items from other cultures, so it was not unusual to find an Orc in Rohan scale-mail, Gondorian steel plate and other items of purloined finery (*above right*).

Shields appear to have been much more prevalent among the Third Age Orcs; again, this may have been Sauron's influence. A better-defended Orc was a longer-surviving Orc, and one that had more chances to kill Sauron's enemies. The shields were principally similar in construction to those of Rohan and Gondor – planks of wood banded together with iron strips riveted into place – but there were also shields of iron plate with a boss roughly beaten into them. Most had iron handgrips behind a boss, and some featured the Eye of Sauron device either carved or beaten into the outer face. Many that were found on the Pelennor Fields were cut into a crescent shape (*left*), which may have served to distinguish their owners as having come from Minas Morgul, formerly Minas Ithil or Tower of the Moon.

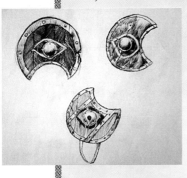

The Nazgûl

THE RED BOOK CONTAINS a full account of their tale, no doubt told by Gandalf, Elrond and others of the Wise, and it is a cautionary tale indeed. The Nazgûl once were Men, great kings in their time and proud; and it was their pride that led to their downfall, for Sauron seduced them with promises of power and immortality. Instead, all they ended up with was suffering and slavery, for once they put on the Rings of Power gifted to them they became in thrall to the Dark Lord, their Ring gradually sucking both body and spirit into itself as a vampire would drain its victim dry. And this slow death would last for as long as Sauron lived.

The Nazgûl, or Ringwraiths as they became known, were Sauron's greatest servants. No ordinary weapon could harm them nor could they be killed by any man. Being born of dark magic, they were allegedly able to freeze their victims into immobility through fear and to inflict the Black Breath, a fatal sickness caused by gazing too long into the faces of one of these dread wraiths or by their touch. Yet they were not invincible, and they were afraid of fire. Perhaps this symbol of the Flame Imperishable, the spirit that moved within the forces of light, was anathema to these creatures of darkness. It appears that Aragorn knew enough about them to use this fear to drive them back from Weathertop when they attempted to seize the Ring-bearer, Frodo Baggins.

During the War of the Ring Sauron used the Nazgûl to travel the length and breadth of Middle-earth in his hunt for the One Ring, and several times they came very close to succeeding. Yet they were thwarted in the Shire, repelled at Weathertop and unhorsed at the Ford of Bruinen; their wraith forms were washed away and were forced to make slow passage back into Mordor. Yet here they were given greater and more terrible steeds with which to continue their master's bidding: Sauron gave them fell beasts to ride. These ancient creatures were

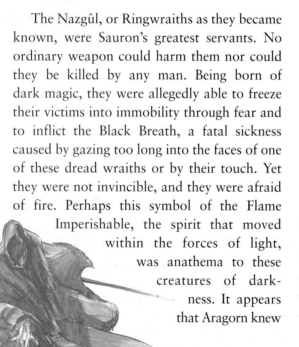

TOP LEFT *Replica of a Nazgûl crown, apparently visible only when in their twilight form (right).*
TOP RIGHT *The Nine were given black horses with which to hunt for the Ring.*
LEFT *Third Age sketch of a Ringwraith closing in on its victim.*

THE WITCH-KING

Chief and greatest among the Nazgûl was the Witch-king of Angmar; to him was given the first of the nine Rings of Power. Writings discovered among Saruman's papers declare that the Rings given to Men were, alone of all the Rings of Power, silver, set with a single amber stone, but those worn by the Nazgûl were withered in size, and the amber stone was red, like an eye. Alone of them, the Witch-king's was of silver and gold, to reflect his elevated status, and the stone was of untainted amber.

Replica of one of the Nazgûl's Rings of Power, corrupted by Sauron's malice.

tireless and could range far, and they were deadly adversaries for the Men of Gondor, as they could swoop down upon infantry and cavalry alike, snatching them up and tearing them to pieces. During the Siege of Gondor they harried the White City's defenders, plucking them from the ramparts and dropping them to their doom, and used their mounts to tear apart the trebuchets. Despite many arrows fired in their direction the Nazgûl and their mounts proved unassailable. When Aragorn led his army to the Black Gate the Nazgûl were part of the host that attacked them there, but they were commanded by Sauron to fly to Mount Doom when he perceived what was about to happen. Yet despite their great speed they were too late, and perished in the inferno caused by their master's destruction.

great indeed, and may be explained by the fact that Sauron's power was waxing as the Ring approached the place of its making. The Witch-king was commander of the forces that marched on Minas Tirith, and he slew Théoden, king of the Rohan, but was himself slain by Théoden's niece, Éowyn. Prophecy had decreed that no Man would kill him, and like all prophecies it came true in ways unlooked for, when the blades of a woman and a hobbit ended the unnatural life of Sauron's greatest servant.

It was the Witch-king who wounded Frodo on Weathertop with a Morgul-knife, and it was he who faced Gandalf at the Siege of Gondor and bested him in single combat by breaking his staff. His might would have been

WEAPONS

It is possible that the Nazgûl carried the swords that had been their royal weapons when they were still Men, although these may have been forged for them in Mordor's armory. They would have been kingly blades, all unique, made by the finest swordsmiths; all were said to be longswords, most with long handgrips allowing them to be wielded with either one or both hands. Their guards and pommels had the brutal jagged lines found in all things of Mordor make; the pommels' coronels and spikes were ugly mockeries of crowns. One sword featured a finger-guard in its ricasso, an unusual feature that spoke of an elegant fighting style learned in ancient times; its position just in front of the guard would have demanded a classic fencing grip that would have kept the blade aligned with the arm, maximizing reach when thrusting. There was evidently enough substance to the Nazgûl to require them to wear armor and allow them to wield their swords, but not enough to maintain their weapons. During the long centuries they had become rusted and pitted, yet their craftmanship meant that they were still formidable blades, and the fact that they were wielded by creatures born of dark magic may have imbued them with a destructive power seen nowhere else.

The Witch-king's sword was similar to the other Nazgûl's: a longsword of some sixty inches including a fourteen-inch, two-handed grip with coronelled pommel – its guard etched with the poisonous weed pattern that appeared on Sauron's mace and armor. He also carried a Morgul-knife, probably about sixteen inches long, which inflicted a mortal wound on Frodo; like all blades made in Morgul's foul armories it dissolved once it had bitten into flesh, leaving the embedded fragment to make its way to the victim's heart. When the Witch-king rode to Minas Tirith on his fell beast he carried with him a great black mace. This he used to smash Gandalf the White's staff and assault King Théoden, but despite its eldritch power he was unable to vanquish Éowyn, who defeated him on the field of battle.

ARMOR

Like the swords, the Nazgûl's armor would have been fit for a king, of the highest-caliber steel and designed to offer the best defense. Although the plates and lames were similarly rusted they still would have offered significant protection.

Each Nazgûl wore a full suit of plate, its spiked design brutally elegant and intimidating, comprising cuirass, pauldron, rerebrace, couter, vambrace and articulated gauntlets made from more than three dozen separately crafted lames; each leg was fully enclosed by cuisse, poleyn, greave and sabaton. Apparently, no helmet was worn, although this will never be known for sure; perhaps somewhere in the void they wore their kingly crowns still. The Witch-king's armor was even more elaborate than that of the other Nazgûl, the ridges and fans of the pauldrons resembling dragon's wings, the spiked couters like spurs, and the heavy gauntlets covered with numerous interlocking lames that were like scales.

169

FELL BEASTS

Little was known of these dread creatures at the time of the War of the Ring, so their appearance would have been awful indeed, doubly so because they carried on their scaly backs the Nazgûl. It is now thought that they were bred by Sauron in desolate eyries that lay in the shadow of the Ash Mountains: this area in Mordor's northern region of Lithlad is now known as the Vale of the Fell Beasts. These winged monsters were one of the Dark Lord's most terrible creations, an unholy alliance of dragon and serpent that could be ridden only,

so it is said, by one directly under the will of Sauron himself. They fed on carrion, devouring the carcasses of horses, men, oxen and Orcs; their piercing shrieks were enough to freeze a man and his mount, their terror rendering them immobile while the great creature plunged down upon them. The beasts were apparently dead gray in color, although some claim they glittered with a purple iridescence. Their scaly bodies had a row of venomous spines running down their backs, and they were reputed to measure at least one hundred feet in length, their batlike wings spanning this and more. When closing in on their prey they would bring their powerful legs forward, the three great claws on each foot flexed, ready to tear into the victim's flesh. The fell beast of the Witch-king was fitted with a spiked iron helmet and face-plate, probably because he expected to be taking it into close-quarter action. It appears that Sauron bred these creatures only as steeds for his Nazgûl, as the nine were the only ones ever seen, their kind disappearing for ever when their creator was destroyed.

ABOVE *Death mask of a fell beast.*
RIGHT *Claw unearthed from land near Mordor.*
BELOW *Some say the Witch-king was a match for Gandalf.*

The Siege of Gondor

A SUCCESSION OF WARS against invading Easterlings and Haradrim, frequent sorties by the Orcs of Mordor, and a devastating plague had steadily reduced Gondor's population so that by the end of the Third Age it was a shadow of what it once had been. Outlying border garrisons were left unmanned, and enemies had encroached into the now sparsely populated lands.

Yet as Gondor diminished so did Mordor grow. Sauron built great engines of war, amassed legions of Orcs and sent his emissaries out to make alliances with Men of the East and South: he would have spent decades planning what would be a final, overwhelming assault upon the White City; once that fell, Middle-earth would be his for the taking.

Yet Sauron had one major problem: Osgiliath was the crossing point on the River Anduin, and any siege equipment and troops that he wanted to use first had to be transported across the river. However, all the bridges of Osgiliath had been destroyed during the past few years of the war, save one that was badly damaged. Therefore, the first part of his strategy would have been to overwhelm the defenders of Osgiliath by driving them back and to use the day or two that he had before Gondor could mount a counterattack to send his Orcs across the river on rafts to attack the western shore where Faramir's Rangers were. Once the western side had been secured, Orc sappers would have made makeshift repairs to the broken bridges, putting very crude platforms across them so the siege towers and catapults could be hauled over and across to the Pelennor Fields. So the capturing of Osgiliath was a critical part of the strategy. The assault that Boromir repelled in

the summer of TA 3018 was clearly the first move: if the Orcs had gained the city then, it is unlikely that the Ring-bearer would ever have made it into Mordor, perhaps not even as far as Rivendell. Yet Osgiliath was eventually taken and held early in TA 3019, and Sauron's army began its invasion of Gondor.

There were several armies of Orcs now in Mordor: the first marched out tens of thousands strong from Minas Morgul under the command of the Witch-king, and they

ABOVE *Authentic campaign map recovered from an Orc corpse.*

The Red Book tells of a huge army of Orcs and trolls that issued out of Minas Morgul, watched over by the Witch-king.

joined with those that had come through the Black Gate, escorting the mountain-trolls and siege towers. Like a herald of woe, a great mass of dark thunderclouds swept out from the east, casting a great shadow over the lands and defenders of Gondor.

The advance of Mordor's army was slowed by Osgiliath, but once through that bottleneck they spread out, forming regiments at least ten ranks across and fifteen deep, each one holding as many as five thousand Orcs, many carrying burning torches in the premature twilight. Crude banners on which were painted the red Eye of Sauron were held proudly aloft, swaying like red trees among the forest of fires. The front regiments were filled with thousands of Orc archers, positioned closest to the battlements where they would be most effective. Moving through the Orc regiments, teams of mountain-trolls pushed huge siege towers filled with Orcs while others steered heavy wheeled catapults closer to the outer wall of the city. Riding up and down the regiments were Orc-captains mounted on Wargs; on these swift creatures they could take their orders from Gothmog, a hideously disfigured Orc chieftain in charge of troop movements on the ground, and shout them quickly and efficiently to their troops. And in the midst of all, troll drummers beat time. To the Orcs it must have sounded like a clock ticking down to victory; to the defenders it must have sounded like the voice of doom.

In those ancient times, the size, weight and area of ground covered by this mass of siege towers and catapults, combined with the noise

Sauron's army that marched on Minas Tirith was said to be 200,000 strong.

The Men of Gondor were driven from the battlements by Nazgûl on fell beasts.

produced by these vehicles as they advanced, the roar of hundreds of wheels rolling over rough ground toward the White City, would have done much to demoralize the defenders before the conflict even began. Even worse, though, would have been the sight of some two-hundred thousand Orcs and Easterlings steadily closing the five-mile distance between Osgiliath and Minas Tirith. All that stood between them and the pitifully few defenders was the outer wall and Great Gate. Men quailed, but had nowhere to run. Gazing upon the approaching army for the first time, Denethor lost his tenuous grip on sanity, so Gandalf the White assumed command of the city, ordering men back to their posts.

After the rout of her knights, Gondor's defense was wisely conducted from within the walls of the city. It would have been futile to face the Orcs on the battlefield. Part of the city's construction had included the installation of many trebuchets, each one placed at the top of towers spaced along the walls of the lower four levels, allowing the defenders to fire down upon any part of the Pelennor Fields. Without these, the city would be almost defenseless. Gradually, the huge army came to a halt just within catapult range.

It was Mordor that threw down the gauntlet, but when its catapults launched an opening salvo it was not rocks but a more terrible

Countless Orcs were slain trying to break through the Great Gates.

missile by far that came tumbling over the walls. This atrocity prompted Gandalf to give the order to return fire, and scores of trebuchets launched boulders down upon the enemy. Years of training allowed them to reload and fire again and again; soon several siege towers were destroyed and countless Orcs were crushed. Elsewhere, Gondorian and Orc archers traded hundreds of arrows, turning the air black. Now the trolls that crewed the siege towers began loading heavy boulders into them, and so began an exchange of heavy missiles that wrought destruction within the city and throughout Sauron's army.

Gondor's defenses were holding their own, and the damage they were inflicting kept the vast horde at bay, but then the Nine Nazgûl plunged out of the sky, emitting piercing shrieks that sent men fleeing from the battlements in terror despite their captains' orders to hold. They swooped down on those remaining and used their fell beasts as flying battering rams to smash the trebuchets into matchwood.

This terrifying distraction allowed the trolls to finally wheel the remaining siege towers up to the sixty-foot-high outer wall, and Orcs brought up a battering ram with which to beat on the gates. Although the gates were impervious to this assault, and hundreds of Orcs were

slain by the arrows that rained down upon them, it served to pull men away from other posts. Then the siege towers unleashed their foul cargo; drawbridges dropped open, smashing down upon the battlements, and scores of Orcs poured forth, swarming over the Gondorian defenders. A furious melee began, as the soldiers desperately tried to keep the Orcs at bay. With every hour that passed another siege tower reached a different part of the wall; mountains of corpses from both sides began to pile up, but so far the defenses were just about holding.

As day turned to dusk, and soldiers raced back and forth to the place where the latest siege tower had reached, Mordor's greatest weapon finally made its way toward the city: Grond, a massive iron battering ram in the form of a ravening wolf some 150 feet long, which was hauled by four great beasts of unknown

origin. Atop the sixty-foot posts burned iron braziers, and Orcs crawled all over it. It was so large and heavy that it had evidently been outpaced by the rest of the army; this may explain why a second battering ram was carried to the siege. Sauron knew that it might be some time before the iron monster arrived and wanted to try to break through as soon as possible. Seeing Grond gradually lumber up toward the city invigorated the Orcs, and they renewed their assault; now the catapults began firing boulders that had been covered in pitch and set alight. With night now fully upon the city, Grond was hauled into position and eight mountain-trolls began swinging the enormous battering ram on its heavy chains. With the first boom of impact a vibration ran through the entire city, and it was not long before the Great Gates splintered under Grond's mighty weight; the snarling wolf's head now leered down upon the terrified defenders in the streets of the first level. Within moments the gate was smashed open completely and trolls poured into the city, closely followed by Easterling warriors.

As flaming boulders continued to crash down upon the lower levels, Gandalf led several hundred Gondorian soldiers through the flames and choking smoke into the midst of the invaders, and furious hand-to-hand combat ensued. Yet despite their bravery they were

As siege towers rolled toward the city, flaming boulders crashed down upon it.

The fiery assault was relentless.

driven back to the second level, and eventually retreated to the third. Now, they were forced to fire their trebuchets down upon the lower levels of their own city, sending flaming debris into the enemy hordes below. It was at this time that the Witch-king flew into the city and faced its commander, Gandalf.

With much of the lower levels aflame and their commander possibly about to fall, Gondor would have suffered its most catastrophic defeat if not for the arrival of the Riders of Rohirrim. History of five hundred years earlier repeated itself as horns sounded and the Men of Rohan came to the aid of the Men of Gondor. Seeing that their right flank was now under attack, the forces of Mordor halted their attempt to gain the upper levels and withdrew to aid their cohorts. This allowed the city's defenders to regroup and repel the invaders, regaining control of the lower levels. The siege was over; the battle had begun.

With the gates in ruins, the rest of Sauron's army closed in upon the city.

Grond & Other Siege Equipment

Saruman's assault on Helm's Deep heralded a new age of warfare in Middle-earth. Before this it had been an age in which success or defeat was in the hands of the individual. Now, the times would begin to change: it would become an age of machines, of weapons that could blindly destroy a mass of individuals with one strike. Saruman's bombs were just the first of many devices that would follow. Fortunately for Gondor, Sauron was not so advanced in thinking as his so-called ally, for a part of him still belonged to an age of antiquity and elegance that resulted in an almost preindustrial approach to warfare. Thus his engines of war were grandiose and infernal but still on the same technological level as those that defended against him. With Saruman's explosive powder at his disposal, the outcome could have been very different indeed.

CATAPULTS

Heavy timber catapults were pushed from Mordor by teams of Mountain-trolls and Orcs. Their fifteen-foot-high frames were on wheels and were fitted with a thirty-foot-long arm; at the far end was an iron basket and at the short end a heavy iron counterweight. Because of the catapults' size, only trolls could work them, and it took at least two to lower the arm so that a boulder or fireball could be loaded into the basket. When the arm was released, the weight dropped and the arm swung up into a hefty crosspiece that had been thickly swaddled to absorb the impact and prevent it shattering. The impact sent the boulder skyward as far as 150 yards, more than enough to take it over the outer wall and into the lower levels of the city. Boulders of ten or twenty pounds inflicted heavy damage on the city, but the effect on morale was equally damaging, for the defenders had never experienced such an assault before.

SIEGE TOWERS

Another innovation that Sauron's Orcs brought on to the battlefield was the siege tower. Each of the wooden towers stood some seventy-five feet tall, specifically built to overlook

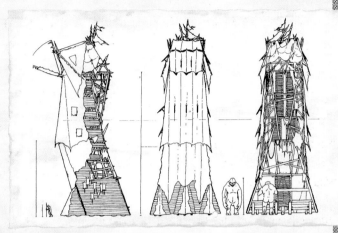

the outer wall of the city, and teemed with Orcs waiting to pour forth. The wheeled towers were fitted inside with ladders that the Orcs used to climb up before the towers were in range of the defenders' arrows. The towers were propelled by teams of mountain-trolls, who had pushed them all the way from the Black Gates. The front of the tower was covered in iron plates to deflect enemy arrows. There was an iron-plated ramp at the front that protected the Orcs inside when raised; once the tower was pushed up to the wall, the ramp would be dropped down onto the battlements,

allowing the Orcs to rush out toward the defenders. Although the towers were highly effective at getting enemy soldiers inside the city wall the critical objective was breaking through the gate. The siege towers didn't ultimately provide a mass penetration of the city because even when they succeeded they were still a vulnerable target and were just a very narrow funnel against which the Gondorian firepower could be channeled. Therefore the siege towers were really there to keep the defenders busy on the walls; the real focus of Mordor's attack was to get through the gate.

GROND

Named after Morgoth's mace, the Hammer of the Underworld, Grond was the largest and most fearsome weapon ever to appear in Middle-earth. It was a battering ram of mighty proportions – said to be 60 feet high and fully 150 feet long – and had been created in the foundries of Mordor for one specific purpose: to break through the seemingly impregnable Great Gates of Minas Tirith. Grond was in the form of a great snarling wolf, whose head, by some magic, glowed with an infernal light. It was suspended from six tall posts by heavy iron chains, above a great iron frame fixed on six spiked iron wheels. Such a monumental contraption would have taken decades to build, so long had Sauron's plan been forming. Yet it proved worthwhile when it smashed through the iron gates with ease, allowing Trolls and Easterlings to pour through the breach.

Sauron would have needed beasts of unsurpassed brute strength to haul Grond from Mordor to Minas Tirith, and it appears that he created them, for the monstrosities that pulled it had never been seen before nor have since. So horrible were these great beasts that accounts differ wildly as to their appearance, some saying they had horns, others tusks, others that they were winged like dragons. Sadly, no true record exists; like many of Sauron's creations, they, like Grond, were unmade at the time of his destruction.

Artists' impressions of how the great weapon might have looked. The scale model, based on the sketch (top), *comes from a private collection.*

Mountain-trolls

MOUNTAIN-TROLLS WERE THE MOST DANGEROUS of all the trolls found in Middle-earth. Unlike their distant cave-dwelling kin they had a basic intelligence and natural cunning and could be trained to perform specific tasks. Moreover, they were unafraid of the sun, as it had no significant effect on them, so they were a menace at all times of the day. Their strength was prodigious, and they were therefore used as beasts of burden as well as for attack. There is still some debate among scholars as to whether the creatures that fought at the Siege of Gondor were true mountain-trolls or rather Olog-hai, a more socialized breed that was somewhere between a troll and an Uruk. At that time, no one had ever witnessed trolls fighting in such an organized fashion, so it is easy to see how the doubt arose.

The height of these creatures was said to be between ten and fifteen feet, on average twice the height of a man. They had the thick arms and two-toed legs of their kind, small wide-set eyes and a protruding lower jaw, out of which jutted large tusks; their scaly gray-brown skin was thicker on the arms, shoulders and back, giving them a natural armor; most unusually, some even had hair and whiskers. Again, this suggests that they were closer to Men than others of their kind. In addition to their calloused skin, many of the trolls were armored with heavy iron plates beaten into lamed pauldrons, spiked pauldrons, breast-plates, greaves and helmets. The brutes were dangerous enough, but they also carried huge clubs and halberds made of wood and iron, which kept all but the bravest or most reckless soldiers at bay. There appear to have been four tasks assigned to the mountain-trolls.

Mordor harnessed the enormous brute strength of the trolls, turning them into beasts of burden and of war.

ATTACK TROLL

Probably the most formidable warriors to come out of Mordor, the attack trolls were trained to use great spiked hammers and halberds in addition to the clubs that were their

traditional weapons. They were not especially agile, but they did have exceptional reach, which is something that their opponents overlooked at their peril. This threat was magnified through their use of staff weapons to stab their opponents while remaining safely out of reach. They swung these from the side, using the axe blade like a scythe or brought them down like an axe. Their weapons were so long that it was only by distraction that a soldier could hope to get inside the troll's reach and strike it. Attack trolls were armored with heavy plate, or occasionally scale, cuirasses, and their arms were protected by vambraces and pauldrons. Their helmets had cheek-plates that extended into spikes, and bars that linked the cheek-plates and brim of the skull to protect them from slashing blows to the face. Their training would have extended no further than getting through the Gates and killing as many Men as possible, but this would have been enough. It is likely that the instruction had the weight of the Dark Lord behind it, or at least one of the Nazgûl, so the trolls would have carried it out as long as they were still standing. Once they were in a battle frenzy, it would have been almost impossible to turn them to another task.

SIEGE TOWER TROLL

Not only were the seventy-five-foot siege towers made of timber but they were also filled with Orcs, so they needed up to four trolls to transport them from Mordor to Minas Tirith.

The trolls carried no arms while pushing the towers, but there may have been weapons stored inside. They wore heavy plates of armor strapped to their torsos and forearms, had spiked pauldrons and wore leather caps to which were riveted leather flaps and iron plates that jutted out over their eyes and cheeks. Protection against missiles from above would have been the primary objective.

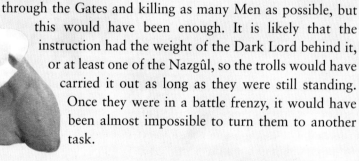

CATAPULT TROLL

The enormous tension under which the catapults operated meant that it would have taken squads of Orcs to do the work of a few trolls, which would have been much slower. Sauron needed his catapults to fire constantly at the White City, so speed and strength were of paramount importance. A pair of trolls could pull down the great arm of the catapult while a third loaded the heavy boulder into the basket, all in the space of a minute or two. These trolls were fitted with wide-brimmed iron helmets that had a spike on top, a visor and leather flaps that protected the troll's eyes from flying missile debris. Their bodies were protected with spiked pauldrons and lamed cuirasses; they carried no weapons, but some were also fitted with an iron vambrace that extended over the hand into a vicious curved claw.

DRUMMER TROLL

Possibly as much for intimidating as for keeping a beat to march to, these trolls carried two large kettle drums hung from their shoulders, which they beat with heavy wooden mallets. The boom from these horsehide-covered drums would have reverberated around the battlefield, its steady beat serving to inspire the Orcs as much as it distressed the Men of Gondor. They were not armored, merely fitted with caps of layers of overhanging hide, shoulder straps of fur and hide and a leather loincloth.

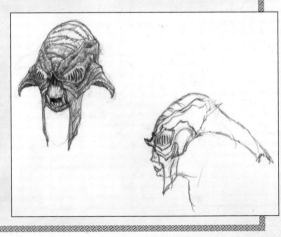

Easterlings

THE EASTERLINGS WERE DESCENDANTS of the Men who had refused to make contact with the Elves during the great western migration early in the Second Age. Instead they remained in the east, establishing a successful confederation of many tribes. They are said to have been a proud people, with a strong hierarchy and caste system that clearly distinguished between the warriors and the servants and workers who looked after them. They were a warlike people; the strong tribes subjugated the weaker ones, often capturing men and women as slaves as far afield as Rhovanion and Khand. By the time of the Third Age, there were traveler's tales claiming that Rhûn was filled with grand cities and splendid temples dedicated to the worship of Morgoth. However, there are no verified accounts of what actually lay in the sterile landscape far to the east of Mordor during the heyday of this conquering people, and now whatever might have stood there has come to dust.

Outwardly, Easterlings were similar in appearance to ordinary Men, apart from their sallow skin, but inwardly they were cruel and loyal servants of Sauron. They had benefited greatly from their alliance with Mordor, which supported their expansionist policy providing they paid tribute to the Dark Lord and served in his army; it is likely that

The Easterlings marched and fought with brutal efficiency, and despite the heat of the eastern lands they were always fully protected by sophisticated metal armor. Their banner was a black and gold serpent against a red field.

had a disciplined combat strategy. They marched and fought in ordered groups using economical moves, and were quick and merciless; during the Siege of Gondor they were sent in after the mountain-trolls when the Great Gates were breached, as Sauron knew that they would be able to quickly and methodically exploit the defenders' disarray, securing the streets on the lower levels. Following Gondor's defeat of Sauron's army, one of the first military offensives conducted by King Elessar was against the surviving Easterlings; under their new king the might of the Free Peoples proved too great and the conquerors were themselves finally conquered.

Sauron would have offered lands in the north of Gondor long desired by them as a reward for such service. He would have greatly valued having such experienced and brutally efficient warriors fighting in his front line, for the Easterlings were seasoned in the art of war and

WEAPONS

The Easterlings had two principal weapons, the polearm and the scimitar. The polearm, fitted with a serrated blade and tipped with a spike, was made in two sizes: the nine-foot polearm was used to defend against enemy charges, particularly from cavalry, while the shorter, five-foot one, featuring spikes at both ends, was used in close combat. Each was backed with a curved spike sharpened on the outer edge: on the long polearm this was used to trip or hamstring enemy horses; on the shorter one it was for piercing armor and deflecting enemy blades. It was a truly versatile weapon that could be used defensively and offensively, offering the Easterling immediate retaliation with a choice of four points of attack. The three-foot-long steel scimitar may have been a recent addition to their arsenal, perhaps an influence from their association with Sauron's Orcs, although the rounded pommel, handgrip and guard cast from a single piece of bronze were clearly of Easterling design. The curved blade was used in a downward, diagonal slashing attack and for thrusting.

ARMOR

Although the Easterling culture was at a high level, and their technology dominant within the region, they were not as advanced as the hated Gondorians. The manufacture of large plates of armor that fit and were consistent demanded a level of sophistication and skill that they did not possess, but they were adept in creating small interlocking lames of bronze that were combined to produce their distinctive jagged scales. The extravagant shapes of the helmet and armor were deliberately intended to intimidate their opponents; it would have been easy to picture them as a swarm of dragons as they descended on their foe. Their bronze armor consisted of a stomach-plate and groin-guard made of riveted plates and lames, a collar, pauldrons, vambraces, cuisses and

greaves; in all, they were extremely well protected, the only weak point being from behind. But because they fought in tight groups, an attack from the rear was not likely. Their armor was inscribed with the strange glyphs of their written language; presumably these were strengthening spells to ward off harm.

The climate of Rhûn was not as hostile as Harad's, but it was evidently fierce enough that their only other clothing was made of light, loose-fitting fabrics dyed red and indigo and black, colors that would have starkly contrasted with the bronze of their armor. The undercut bronze helmet was worn over a headscarf (*left*) and featured cheek- and eye-guards; the three angular crests struck a distinctive and aggressive silhouette that could be recognized from a long way off, intimidating even before battle was commenced.

Like the Haradrim, the Easterlings also wore their family wealth upon them, whether in pieces of bronze or jewels or other ornament. They also liked to wear battlefield trophies, talismans of success that would inspire them to new glory and greater riches and totems of fear that would intimidate their next opponents. The curved rectangular shield had concave top and bottom edges and was held by means of an iron handgrip behind a circular boss that was surrounded by a diamond shape; like the armor, it was inscribed with mysterious symbols. No scholar has succeeded in translating a single glyph, so it appears that the Easterlings' language died with them.

The Battle of the Pelennor Fields

THE LONGEST NIGHT IN GONDOR'S HISTORY was over; with the dawn came the ringing sound of horns, and the sight of six thousand Riders of the Rohirrim on the horizon. Although they had ridden hard for three days since leaving Dunharrow, both horses and riders were ready for battle; the sight of the White City in flames had ignited a fury in them, but in none more so than their king. Théoden gave the order for his riders to form into three companies, and these were led by Éomer on the left flank, Grimbold on the right, nearest the wall, and Gamling in the center, behind the king's banner. Théoden drew Herugrim and rode along the entire line of his Rohirrim, the clattering noise of steel against lance filling the still morning air. It is said that at that moment a single shaft of sunlight broke through the cloud, and the gray-bearded king turned golden, dazzling all who beheld him.

Théoden led from the front, like one of the great heroes of old, and the three companies were hard pressed to keep up with their charismatic and beloved king. In a move similar to that which had rescued him from certain death at the hands of the Uruk-hai, Théoden led his Rohirrim from the northern edge of the Pelennor Fields as they thundered down into the flank of the vast Orc army, estimated to still be about 150,000 strong, that swarmed around the city a mile to the south. So began the greatest battle of the War of the Ring.

Théoden divided his 6,000 Rohirrim into three companies and led them from the front.

None of the besiegers expected to be attacked from anywhere but from within the city. It was widely believed that their ally, Saruman the White Wizard, and his Uruk-hai had annihilated the Men of Rohan, and

The Rohirrim carved a bloody swath through the Orcs.

Mordor's other allies, the Corsairs of Umbar, had destroyed the remaining Men of Gondor in the south; therefore, no provision had been made to protect their flanks.

Whole Orc companies disappeared under the sea of hooves as the six thousand Riders pushed into the main body of the Orc army. Lances were lowered and Orcs were skewered and still the horses rode on, crashing through rank after rank until they were pressed about on all sides. Then swords and axes were drawn, and the field was full of the sound of hacking and slashing as steel met shield and flesh.

So fierce was the onslaught of Rohan that the superior numbers of Orcs were in disarray and began to flee, yet when the tide looked set to turn, another of Mordor's allies took to the battlefield. Twenty mighty mûmakil lumbered forward through a sea of Men and Orcs, driven mercilessly by their brutal Haradrim masters. Goaded into war, the mûmakil bellowed

in anger and swung their great heads from side to side, each of their four long tusks sweeping aside and impaling men and horses as the advancing beasts trampled all under foot. From the war-towers that sat atop the great beasts, scores of Haradrim archers who were packed within sent a rain of arrows down upon the panicked Riders and their mounts. What had seemed like victory suddenly turned into a rout. Desperately, Théoden tried to rally his men, but it was at this point that the Witch-king swept down, his fell beast plucking up both horse and rider before dropping them to their death.

As the Witch-king hovered above the dying king, ready to let his mount feed, a solitary soldier beheaded the beast, sending the Nazgûl toppling to the ground. The Witch-king rose and launched into a powerful attack upon the figure, who was on the point of being defeated when the soldier revealed herself as Éowyn, daughter of kings. The thain's book recalls that sight of the fair maiden gave the Lord of the Nazgûl pause, which was enough for Merry to plunge his sword not once but twice into the leg of the Witch-king. While he was fatally distracted, Éowyn delivered the killing blow, and he who could be killed by no man fell. It was an act of unparalleled heroism and significance, but it went unnoticed by all in the chaos of battle, as mûmakil battered the outer

INSET OPPOSITE *Color study of the Army of the Dead washing over the Orc army.*
BELOW *The Pelennor Fields in times of peace.*

Their onslaught was too great to withstand.

wall of the city unmolested and the Rohirrim lay all-but destroyed.

For those trapped within the White City the sight of ten black-sailed Corsair ships now pulling into the river port and docks of Harlond would have looked like the end, but it was not a pirate that stepped forth but a king. Aragorn leapt from the gunwale toward the waiting Orcs as if he had an army of thousands at his back instead of just an Elf and a Dwarf, which must have amused the Orcs greatly, as they would have been expecting

their allies from the south. What they got instead was a spectral army of some five thousand Dead Men who had finally come to honor their oath to the king of Gondor. Accounts of what happened are contradictory; some even maintain that the Dead never walked the Pelennor Fields at all, but some say that they surged out like a rolling wave, sweeping over the Orcs and up the mûmakil in a rage of bloodlust. Those that were not slain fled in terror: their weapons could not touch these apparitions while the Dead could kill with a touch. Eventually the field of battle was silent; the Dead had fulfilled their duty and were at last released by the king to find their rest. Despite all the odds, Gondor had defeated the superior might of Mordor. The war was not over, but the battle had been won.

Haradrim

THE PRIMITIVE AND SAVAGE PEOPLE of Harad lived in one of the harshest environments in Middle-earth. In the land south of Gondor the sun beat down unrelentingly, cooking much of Harad's great plains into desert. The tribes of Haradrim lived a nomadic existence, walking from one oasis to another in search of precious water and food, and here they would gather kine and other beasts. Farther south in Far Harad there were said to be dense jungles, in which was found a bamboo-like material that they used for weapons, armor, utensils and construction; the desert lands of Harad yielded few trees, so bamboo was used in place of wood. Their metal-working technology was almost nonexistent due to lack of natural resources; they relied heavily on organic materials, using tusk, bone and obsidian in place of steel.

In battle they drove their mûmakil into the enemy ranks, causing terror and panic; with their foes in disarray the Haradrim then fired spears and arrows down upon them from the covered frame atop the mûmakil. Usually this would be enough to rout their foe, but if not the main host charged in behind the great beasts, using their spears, swords and bows with bloodthirsty zeal. Tribal leaders wore great spiked ceremonial frames on their backs, adorned with colored stones, cloth, bone, spear tips and other precious items to signify rank.

When Sauron's emissaries visited the tribes, the Haradrim would have needed little persuading to ally with him; Sauron's great skill was knowing how to appeal to people's base desires. He would have offered them Gondor's fertile lands in exchange for their loyalty. Of course, they would have been looking for vengeance, well remembering how the Númenóreans had ruled them mercilessly. Instead, all they found was death; most of Harad's population was wiped out on the Pelennor Fields. With the life literally sucked out of Harad, its threat to Gondor disappeared, and in the Fourth Age it submitted to King Elessar, becoming a southern province of Gondor.

LEFT *The heavy canvas of a mûmak platform protected the warriors.*
ABOVE *Artist's impression of a tribal leader's war frame.*

WEAPONS

The weaponry employed by the Haradrim was dictated by factors such as lack of natural resources and the heat. Ore was so precious that it would not have

been possible to manufacture swords or other heavy blades; any steel weapons they had were probably gotten in trade from the neighboring Easterlings, as was the bronze armor found among some of the wealthier tribes. Instead the Haradrim would have favored bows and spears, which could be used to hunt with. Although the sixty-inch bows would have been made from precious supplies of wood, reinforced with wicker, the arrow and spear shafts, even the quiver, were made from bamboo. Tusk, bone and obsidian were used for the arrowheads and spear tips and coarse black feathers – perhaps crow or even vulture – for the arrows' flights. These roughly made arrows would have had only a limited range and accuracy, perhaps being effective only within a distance of one hundred yards or so. The Haradrim also carried a sword and a cruder version of the spear, which was a pitchfork formed by cutting two spikes into a length of bamboo.

ARMOR

The intense heat ruled out the use of heavy armor; it seems that the level of protection differed among the tribes, with warriors wearing a combination of breastplate, back-plate, and collar. These were all a composite of wicker, bamboo, stone, bone and tusk, all interwoven to form a light yet tough shell. From examples recovered from the Pelennor Fields it appears that the Haradrim also carried their personal wealth upon them, as obsidian, shells, blue and amber beads and even bronze were attached or incorporated into their armor, and beads were carved into skull shapes that may have been totems. When going into battle they often wore masks made from hide, bamboo or bone to further intimidate their enemy. They carried no shields, because the weight would have been too much in the heat; all other "armor" was directed to protecting them from the sun, so coarse, dark red linen covered every inch of their bodies, with the bottom of the robe made of rough strips: even their heads were swathed in thin dark red linen.

Mûmakil

ALONG WITH THE BAMBOO-LIKE PLANT that formed all the Haradrim's equipment, there was another precious discovery made deep within the jungle of Far Harad: the mûmak. To most cultures, the mûmakil, or oliphaunts, were creatures of legend, as fabulous and fearsome as dragons, and to them were ascribed all kinds of strange powers. Fear and superstition went before them, and the Haradrim well understood the advantage to be gained by bringing these huge beasts into battle. Besides being formidable in the actual shock of battle, these monsters inspired terror by their size, their ferocity, and the prevailing ignorance about them.

No complete mûmak skeleton has ever been found, but accounts found in both the Red Book and in other scrolls suggest that they stood between fifty and one hundred feet tall, with four huge tusks and two smaller ones to each side of the mouth. When charging into battle, they bellowed and screeched at great volume, and the advent of their coming was preceded by a thunderous din that shook the very earth.

Virtually nothing is known about how the Haradrim succeeded in capturing and taming this monster, let alone how they managed to

Mûmakil were true monsters, the largest beasts ever to walk the face of Middle-earth.

attach the great bamboo and canvas war harness to its back: presumably they were able to coerce it into kneeling or lying down so that a team could haul the huge framework into place, tying it under the belly of the beast. Hanging from the harness were ropes that the Haradrim used to climb up into the frame and take up their positions on platforms. Their elevated position allowed them to target an otherwise hidden enemy and gave their arrows and spears increased range. Gondorian folklore of the time maintains that a shaman, who steered the mûmak using long reins, was the means by which the beast was tamed in the first place. Long banners were hung from the frame, their red and black colors depicting the Eye of Mordor and the snake of the east.

Among the tribes of Haradrim, a mûmak would have been, literally, a huge status symbol, and there would have been great competition among the tribes to possess one; it is likely that this competition led to frequent tribal wars. The mûmakil would have moved with the tribes as they traveled across the desert, which would have been quite often; something as big as a mûmak would soon have exhausted the available resources. A dead mûmak was almost as valuable as a living one, as it would have provided the tribe with a mountain of resources: tusks, bone, hide, dyes, sinew and meat that could be salted, keeping the tribe in food for months; even its dung would have been used for firewalls and packing their temporary homes. It is said that a mûmak could be killed with a single shot to the eye; otherwise it would be able to withstand an onslaught against its thick hide before eventually falling. After their destruction at the hands of the Dead Men of Dunharrow, mûmakil were never again seen in the fertile lands of Middle-earth.

RIGHT *Haradrim banner, with the Eye of Sauron and the snake of the Easterlings.*
BELOW *Felling a mûmak required hundreds of arrows, or just one perfect shot.*

191

The Corsairs of Umbar

URING THE KIN-STRIFE that led to Gondor's costly civil war, a great many of its invincible navy supported the usurper, who was challenging the king's right to rule the country. Eventually he was overthrown and the rightful king restored to the throne, driving the rebels to found their own province and declare themselves under self-rule. Initially these sailors were based in the Gondorian port of Pelargir, but eventually they withdrew to the more southerly haven of Umbar, which sat on the northern coast of Harad. Over time these sailors drew to their number various outlaws and brigands from outlying settlements surrounding the Anduin, and they took to raiding along the coastline of southern Gondor, intercepting merchant vessels and abducting women to bolster their dissident community. They were also slavers and would often seize a ship's crew along with her cargo; if any resisted he would be thrown overboard. Ever after these slaves would spend their lives pulling oars on the corsairs' great black ships.

The corsairs were a thorn in Gondor's side and were partly responsible for its impoverished state, restricting as they had its trade with other realms. Beyond the obvious desire for wealth, there would initially have been some motivation to strike against a kingdom which the corsairs saw as compromised; later it would have been just about greed. The crew of a corsair ship was said to be a mixed bag, generally swarthy and unkempt but garbed in gaudy clothing and jewelry; some would have had an exotic look born of their Southron ancestry.

The corsairs had just one battle strategy, but it was one that had served them well through many centuries: they would use their superior nautical abilities and vastly superior ships to outpace and outmaneuver their victims until they had pulled alongside; then they would launch harpoons from the iron crossbows fixed port and starboard on their ship, anchoring it to the other vessel. As the two ships closed, a raiding party would launch a volley of arrows into the crew if they showed any signs of resistance, before leaping across and seizing control of the vessel. Usually, the corsairs' fearsome reputation would have been enough to intimidate all but the bravest crew, regardless of the value of the cargo.

Sauron would have realized just how useful the corsairs could be to him, so his emissaries would have enlisted their support, possibly making treaties with them after passing through Harad.

Rare pencil study of two corsairs. Little else exists to show what the pirates of the south actually looked like.

Needless to say, the greater part of their inducement to aid Sauron would have been the promise of booty from the White City. By having them raid the various settlements that were situated along the coast, right up to Minas Tirith, Sauron would have gained an intimidating southern front that would need to be defended against, thus drawing away a precious number of Gondor's soldiers. The corsairs' raids would have been damaging in other ways: to see smoke rising from the southern villages and the telltale silhouette of the great ships' sails would have been deeply demoralizing for the defenders within the White City, weakening them even before battle commenced. Furthermore, once the corsairs had moored at Harlond they would have provided reinforcements for Sauron's army if required; they could have provided useful transport up and down the river for his troops or plundered equipment should the battle have been won by the time they arrived.

CORSAIR SHIP

There appear to have been ten of the great ships under the control of the corsairs. These behemoths were said to be 450 feet long and 45 feet in the beam, although these estimates have never been confirmed, as none of the ships survive; the three tall masts each supported an enormous crimson sail, the largest of which may have been fully 400 feet high. Their angular fan shape would have cut a distinctive and terrifying silhouette in the water. Once they were visible it was probably already too late. Yet the most frightening facet of the ships was never seen, only felt; just below the waterline sat a huge iron battering ram, its jagged edges extending perhaps fifty feet out from the keel.

The elegant curving jagged lines of this ram and the rest of the ironwork revealed the ships to be clearly of Númenórean design, especially in the defensive rows of iron spikes that ran from prow to stern on each side. Secured to the hull behind these with iron brackets was a wall of red wooden shields that would have made it almost impossible for anyone to storm the deck. The deck was fitted fore and aft with a pair of iron-framed crossbows that fired harpoons to which were attached grappling lines that bit deep into the victim's hull; once these were embedded, the merchant ship would be stuck fast and vulnerable. A brazier was kept stoked next to the crossbows for the time when the corsairs set light to the other ship, usually just after it had been emptied of its cargo.

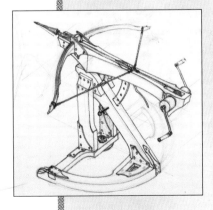

The corsair ships were biremes, in that they were fitted port and starboard with two rows of oars; each row had twenty-one oars and required a minimum of three men per oar; this meant that more than 250 slaves would have been chained below deck. Rowing would have been an exhausting task and would have resulted in a high turnover of slaves; in order to continue raiding, the corsairs would have needed to keep slaving, a vicious circle that terrorized the people of Gondor.

The Dead Men of Dunharrow

WHEN ELENDIL AND GIL-GALAD SENT OUT a call to arms, summoning all good Men and Elves to join the final assault against Sauron's army, most kingdoms and tribes of Men responded by sending their warriors to Gondor. There was one tribe from the White Mountains, however, that promised to come but never showed. History does not recall the reason for this betrayal, only the outcome: this tribe of Men was cursed by Isildur never to have rest while their oath to Gondor remained unfulfilled. They would walk the earth in suffering and shame until they died, and then they would walk the earth as wraiths, ghastly decomposed and skeletal specters consumed by the pain of their humiliation. They hid themselves away in the dark passages of the Dwimorberg mountain, seeking the illusion of a tomb, even if that customary state of rest had been denied them.

No one seeking to travel the path under the mountain that divided Rohan and Gondor ever emerged, so it became known as the Haunted Pass. No one, that is, until Aragorn, accompanied by Legolas and Gimli, sought the aid of this Army of the Dead. It is recounted in the Red Book that by his sword, Andúril, the king of the Dead, knew Aragorn to be the true king of Gondor, and agreed to honor the three-thousand-year-old oath. Aragorn led them first to the River Anduin, where they captured a fleet of Corsair ships that had been raiding the coast; these they sailed up to Harlond, the harbor and quay at the southern perimeter of the Pelennor Fields.

It is not known how these wraiths engaged and killed the enemy once they got to the

ABOVE *The northern entrance to the Dwimorberg lay near Dunharrow.*
LEFT *The City of the Dead was said to fill the inside of the mountain.*

Pelennor Fields, as accounts are vague and contradictory. But most suggest that although the Dead Men's weapons appeared to pass through their victims with no resistance, the effect was that of a real weapon. Similarly, if one of them traveled through an enemy or reached into him, the effect was instantaneous. The Army of the Dead swept across the battlefield killing Orc, mûmak, Easterling and Haradrim alike, leaving none alive. Their oath at last fulfilled, the Dead Men were allowed by Aragorn to finally depart Middle-earth.

WEAPONS

The Dead Men of Dunharrow belonged to a culture that predated Rohan and Gondor, one that appears to have developed its own subtle variant motifs, such as the vulture, which appeared on the noseguard of their helmets and within the architecture of their necropolis. However, there was evidently still a fundamental need for the same type of weaponry as the Men of Rohan and Gondor used. Among the various so-called firsthand accounts of those who witnessed the Army of the Dead take to the battlefield on that famous day in March, TA 3019, there are reports that they carried longswords, axes and spears.

These same accounts say that the Dead Men glowed with a sick green phosphorescence, and when they attacked, they surged and rolled over the thralls of Mordor in successive vaporous waves, screaming an unearthly scream as they came. The specters moved faster than their enemy could run, and when they swung their weapons they left a trail of vapor behind them. Strangest and most horrific of all, it is alleged by some witnesses that, instead of drawing blood from their victims, the Dead Men's weapons seemed to suck the very life out of them. Perhaps fear was a more deadly weapon for them than iron ever could be.

ARMOR

The armor worn by the Dead Men appears to have been reasonably sophisticated for the time, about the same level as that worn by the Rohan some three thousand years later: combinations of mail hauberks, steel plates and helmets reinforced with cheekplates and noseguards.

The king himself is said to have worn a cuirass made of a lattice of interlacing leather straps and a cloak of pure red, a noble garment that was the only point of color in the spectral sea. Of course, by the time of their recall to the war against Sauron, these men had long since passed the point of needing armor; no weapon save that of the King of Gondor could have harmed them or impeded them in their annihilation of the army of Mordor.

The Siege of Gondor/Battle of the Pelennor Fields battle plan

1. Orcs pour out of Minas Morgul and swarm into Osgiliath; they quickly overrun the Gondorian garrison defending it.
2. The main Orc army, tens of thousands strong, marches alongside Easterlings and mountain-trolls pushing great siege towers and catapults. The army stops just within catapult range.
3. Mordor's catapults fire an opening salvo over the city

walls. The defenders respond by launching countless boulders down upon their foe. A heavy missile exchange ensues, destroying siege towers and setting the city aflame.

4. Nazgûl swoop down on the battlements, destroying trebuchets and seizing men.
5. The Nazgûl assault allows siege towers to reach the outer wall and a small battering ram to reach the

gate. Scores of Orcs pour out of the towers, and furious fighting breaks out along the wall.

6. Grond is hauled up to the Great Gates; mountain-trolls swing the enormous battering ram and soon the great wolf's head smashes through. Trolls and Easterlings swarm through into the first level; desperate hand-to-hand fighting ensues.

7. The Gondorians are driven back to the third level; Gandalf faces the Witch-king astride his fell beast.

8. The 6,000 Riders of Rohan arrive. Forming three columns, they charge down, cutting a huge swath through the disordered Orc ranks.

9. The Haradrim lead their mûmakil into the fray, causing panic among the Rohirrim. The Witch-king's fell beast swoops down, mortally wounding King Théoden. Éowyn, aided by Merry, battles the Witch-king.

10. The black ships of the Corsairs of Umbar arrive. Aragorn leads out the Army of the Dead, who annihilate the terrified enemy. The allies win the day!

The Black Gate of Mordor

N AMED MORANNON BY THE SINDARIN ELVES, its translation was "black gate," and it was the main entrance into Mordor. The Black Gate was set in an impregnable black stone and iron wall that stretched from the Mountains of Ash in the north to the Mountains of Shadow in the west. The wall has been estimated to have been 60 feet high and 250 feet wide with each half of the great gate being 90 feet wide and set on large stone wheels. Behind the gate were circular stone ramparts, and when the gate needed to be opened two pairs of moun-

tain-trolls who were tethered to gigantic beams pushed their way around their rampart's track, gradually

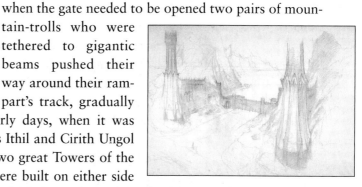

levering open the gate. In Gondor's early days, when it was building towers and cities such as Minas Ithil and Cirith Ungol close to Mordor's border, it raised the two great Towers of the Teeth, Narchost and Carchost, which were built on either side of the wall and were tall enough to overlook it. In those days they prevented anything from entering or leaving the black land, but eventually, as with most of Gondor's outposts, the watch failed and they were taken over by servants of Sauron.

During the latter half of the Third Age, Sauron had been amassing tens of thousands of Orcs in preparation for his plan to conquer Middle-earth, and the force that marched on Minas Tirith was but one of several armies at his disposal. In fact, the greater part of his

troops, estimated at three hundred thousand, remained within Mordor waiting to be com-

ABOVE *View of a slag hill, looking west from the Black Gate.*
ABOVE RIGHT *Sketch of the Morannon, believed to be authentic.*
RIGHT *The watch on the gate was said never to sleep.*

manded to fight; these were gradually being rounded up and directed to the Black Gate. There is great irony in the fact that when Aragorn used the palantír to let Sauron know that Isildur's heir was leading a host to the Black Gate to challenge him, it prompted the mustering of the last pockets of Orcs, into which Frodo and Sam were drawn. So the gambit designed to be a last diversion to give the hobbits more time nearly resulted in the quest failing within sight of its goal. As is well known, however, the hobbits managed to slip away and reach Mount Doom. There is no doubt that with all the Orcs gathered by the gate their journey would have been more treacherous if the land had been still swarming with the enemy.

Only five hundred soldiers gathered on a slag-hill under the banner of the king (above left).

Aragorn knew that in order to give the hobbits as much of a chance as possible, he had to act immediately, so just two days after reveal-ing himself to Sauron he led out the remains of the armies of Rohan and Gondor, united under the banner of the king, and took them to within sight of the Black Gate. Only five hundred were said to be there that day. Despite the tiny number, Sauron sent out his chief emissary, the lieutenant of the Black Tower, to parley with them. Perhaps this act was intended as a final humiliation to his most feared and hated adversary before he was crushed by the might

Wearing the outfit of the king, Aragorn led his men to the Black Gate.

199

ABOVE *The bright banners of many of the Free Peoples flew outside the Black Gate.*
RIGHT *Brave were the hearts, and strong was the iron.*

of Sauron's host, but Aragorn instead dealt out royal justice to this Mouth of Sauron who had attempted to deceive him with his poisoned words.

After this act there could be only one outcome: drums boomed out of the mountains, fires flared and the great iron gate opened to the sound of tortured metal. As the Men of Rohan and Gondor readied their defense upon two slag-hills, they watched in awe and fear as an endless host of Orcs, trolls and Easterlings poured forth; estimates vary wildly but it appears that two hundred thousand to three hundred thousand surrounded them. With certain death staring them in the eye, the king gave a rousing speech that gave his men the heart to face their end with courage and honor. Yet at the very last when all seemed doomed to fail, the quest was fulfilled and the Ring was unmade, and Sauron and all his works were destroyed. Those of his creatures that were not destroyed fled into the shadows and never attacked Gondor or her allies again. And so ended the War of the Ring.

Aragorn fought like a king and slew a mighty troll.

200

The Mouth of Sauron

THIS UNNAMED SERVANT OF SAURON was said to have once been one of the Dúnedain, a man of the island of Númenor, but like many of his kin he desired power and immortality beyond his allotted span and so turned against the Valar, becoming one of the so-called Black Númenóreans. He came to Middle-earth and settled in Umbar, where, along with others of his kind, he ruled the Haradrim. Like most of the Black Númenóreans, he became corrupted by Sauron during the Second Age and came to hate all of the Free Peoples, especially the descendants of the Faithful and the line of Isildur. In Sauron's service he became a powerful sorcerer, and through his magics greatly extended his life. Because of his evil and his cunning, he quickly rose in position, eventually becoming lieutenant of the Tower of Barad-dûr.

His helm left only his mouth exposed and was etched with runes written in the Black Speech:

"I am the Mouth of Sauron, hear him speak."

Although he carried a sword, his deadliest weapon was made not of metal but of words, and he would use it to devastating effect, killing hope instead of flesh. He may have been directly involved in winning the allegiance of the peoples of the south, although with the once-conquered Haradrim fear may have played as great a part as bribe. His disheveled mount was clothed much as he was, in a combination of dirty rags and rough spiked armor, much of which was rusting through neglect.

His final parley was with Aragorn, who concluded negotiations in decisive fashion, proving that his weapon was stronger than his opponent's.

Aragorn

AT THE TIME OF THE WAR OF THE RING, Aragorn (TA 2931 – FO 120), son of Arathorn, was the last in a long unbroken line stretching back to Isildur, the last king of Gondor. During his early years, following his father's death at the hands of hill-trolls, his newly widowed mother, Gilraen, gave him the name Estel, meaning "hope," to conceal his true identity from the emissaries of Sauron, who were searching for the last descendant of the kings of the Dúnedain. She took him to Rivendell, and he was raised by Lord Elrond himself. At the age of twenty Elrond revealed to Aragorn his true name and ancestry and gave him the heirlooms of the royal line: the Ring of Barahir and the shards of Elendil's sword, Narsil. Under Elrond's guidance, Aragorn became wise beyond his years, and as thoughtful and learned in lore as he was skilled in combat. His Ranger's tracking abilities were among the finest in Middle-earth. Under the name of Thorongil he served many lords in the fight against Mordor, including Théoden's father, Thengel, and Denethor's father, Ecthelion. He also befriended Gandalf and served him well by tracking the elusive creature Gollum across Middle-earth intermittently for thirteen years before finally capturing him in TA 3017.

Although it would have been his royal privilege, Aragorn chose not to carry with him the shards of Narsil as a sign of his high ancestry. It is well known that he was burdened with doubt that he would be strong enough to face the challenges that lay ahead of him, should he choose to take up the mantle of king that was rightfully his. He well knew the failing of his ancestor, Isildur, that had led to such straitened times. Instead of renown, Aragorn sought anonymity and worked always in the shadows for the good of

ABOVE *The young Estel was given the heirlooms of his line: the Ring of Barahir, the shards of Narsil, and his true name, Aragorn.*
LEFT *Aragorn became one of the greatest hunters of his age.*

Aragorn was eighty-eight years old when he rode out to challenge Sauron.

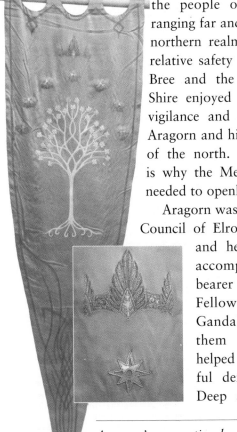

the people of Middle-earth, ranging far and wide across the northern realms. Much of the relative safety that the Men of Bree and the hobbits of the Shire enjoyed was due to the vigilance and fighting skill of Aragorn and his fellow Rangers of the north. (This protection is why the Men of Bree never needed to openly bear arms.)

Aragorn was a member of the Council of Elrond at Rivendell, and he volunteered to accompany the Ring-bearer as part of the Fellowship; following Gandalf's fall, he led them in Moria. He helped lead the successful defense of Helm's Deep and later raised the Dead Men of Dunharrow to aid Gondor, leading them on to the Pelennor Fields in Gondor's hour of greatest need. Following this victory he rode to the Black Gates at the head of a column of just five hundred men, hoping to lure Sauron out in a final, last-ditch attempt to distract the Dark Lord's Eye from the two hobbits.

Following the victory of the Free Peoples of Middle-earth, Aragorn was finally crowned king of Gondor. He then married his beloved Arwen. During his 120-year reign he reclaimed all of Gondor's lands that had been lost, and established the reunited kingdom of Arnor and Gondor; when Aragorn died he was 210 years old, and the crown passed to his son, Eldarion.

Aragorn's coronation banner, with the crown and seven stars, presented to him by his bride, Arwen. The exquisite crown worn by Aragorn once belonged to his ancient ancestor Isildur.

203

WEAPONS

Although a Ranger, Aragorn carried a warrior's sword: nearly five feet long, its narrow fullered blade was four feet from steel cross-guard to sharply tapered tip. This gave the blade a powerful combination of strength, reach and speed. The shape of the blade suited Aragorn's style of fighting, which had been strongly influenced by his Elven upbringing. More than other Men, he used his acute sense of balance and exceptional hand-eye coordination to outmaneuver his opponents, using the strength of their blow against them by taking the blow high up in their swing and redirecting it, using the length of his blade. Once off-balance, his foes were vulnerable to his lightning-fast counterattack, which normally would have been two-handed. The sword also gave him the superior reach to thrust past an enemy's defense using a one-handed strike. Because of its length, the sword had a long handgrip bisected by a steel ring, so that it could be gripped with either one or two hands depending on the method of attack, and the blade was counter-balanced by a large scent-bottle-shaped pommel. The scabbard was plain but had wrapped to it under the leather covering a small second scabbard that contained a utility knife, which would have been used for day-to-day tasks such as skinning animals, cutting wood for kindling, cutting twine and rawhide for repairs and other sundry chores.

BOW

Aragorn also carried with him a small bow of dark-stained wood, about three feet long, which would have been used more for hunting than as a range weapon. It was a shortbow but was not composite in construction; instead it was like a miniature version of the Gondorian longbow, with a subtle curve introduced into the stave during its man-ufacture. The string would have been held under high tension, so Aragorn would have carried the bow unstrung whenever possible to preserve its effectiveness. The arrows were only about twenty inches long, so the bow could not be fully drawn; this would have meant that it had an effective range of only about 75 yards – although modest, this would have been enough for the stealthy hunter to bring down his prey.

HUNTING KNIFE

When the Fellowship left the Elven kingdom of Lothlórien, Celeborn made a gift to Aragorn of an Elven hunting knife. Like many Elven blades it had sinuous lines reminiscent of a new shoot's growth; the handgrip was made of a hardwood, possibly oak, and the canted pommel was brass. Its beautifully curving blade had the following inscription written down it in stylized Sindarin:

Gud Daedheloth
[Foe of Morgoth's realm]

Being right-handed, Aragorn wore his sword on his left side and his knife at his back; if drawing only one weapon, he would have drawn the sword across his body to release it from the scabbard, but he would have gripped the knife hilt in his fist and drawn it upward, ready to hammer down like a nail into his enemy. When both weapons were drawn, the knife would have been held in the left hand and used to stab and slash like a small sword; by bringing the two blades together in an X he could defend himself from enemy blows, blocking and trapping their weapon before withdrawing the knife and using it to attack the foe, who would now be at close range. The knife was housed in a  leather scabbard fitted with a brass locket and chape that was kept out of the way at the back of the sword belt, suspended by two small leather straps. The belt also carried a whetstone in a small leather holster and a leather pouch containing his travel repair kit of oil, cloth and perhaps grit to rub along the blade to get rid of rust.

ANDÚRIL

Andúril, meaning "flame (or "brilliant light") of the west" in Quenya, was reforged from the shards of Elendil's legendary sword, Narsil, by the smiths of Rivendell and taken to Aragorn at Dunharrow by Lord Elrond himself. There could have been no more potent a symbol than this sword: presented with it thus, Aragorn would have finally accepted that it was his duty and his fate to step forward as the rightful king of Gondor. Yet Elrond's motive lay more in Aragorn using it to rally the Army of the Dead to Gondor's aid, for he knew that without them, it was likely that Sauron's forces would have the victory. All the hopes of Men and Elves rested on this sword, and in Aragorn's belief in its power as a symbol of his right to rule.

Andúril was the same in every respect as Narsil, except for the runic inscription that appeared inside the fuller down the length of the blade. The inscription was Quenya, in the runes of Eregion, and appeared on both sides.

These were framed by stylized symbols of the sun (detailed in amber enamel near the hilt) and the moon (engraved at the narrowest terminus of the fuller) and were interspersed at regular intervals by a total of seven symbolic stars. The stars represented Elendil, who died wielding Narsil in battle against Sauron (where the blade was broken). The sun and moon symbols represented his sons, Anárion and Isildur, respectively.

	The transcription reads:	Which means:
ᚠᚾᚱ	*Anar*	*Sun*
ᛏᚪᛏᛁᚾ ᚠᚪᛉᚲᛁᛏ ᛁ ᛏᚻ ᛏᚾᚲᛁᛁᛏ ᛁ	*Nányë Andúril i né Narsil i*	*I am Andúril who was Narsil the*
ᛒᚾᚲᛁᛏ ᚻᛁᚾᛉᛁᛏᚪ ᛏᚻᚲᚠᛉᚱᚾ	*macil Elendilo. Lercuvanten*	*sword of Elendil. Let the*
ᛏᛏᚻᛏ ᛁ ᛒᛉᚻᛏ ᛒᚪᚲᚠᛉᚲᚻᚪ	*i móli Mordóreo.*	*thralls of Mordor flee me.*
ᛁᛏᛁᛏ	*Isil*	*Moon*

This inscription also appeared on the belt that carried Andúril and, in part, on a steel and brass plate that was fixed to the plain black scabbard.

ARMOR

Like all Rangers, Aragorn avoided metal armor because the weight would have been a hindrance more than a help; similarly, he did not wear a helmet. Instead his outfit consisted of a fine linen shirt (*right*), delicately embroidered, probably made for him at Rivendell, and black woolen hose; the tall boots were of a soft, travel-worn leather. A long leather sleeveless jerkin was worn over the shirt, which was secured with braided cord ties at the front. Over this went a coat of thicker, tougher leather whose sleeves were stitched along the underside of their lengths and at the shoulders; it is probable that these could have been removed if necessary. Aragorn also carried a cloak, which was rolled up on his back when not in use (*opposite bottom left*). He wore this outfit up until the time when he was outfitted in his kingly garb prior to riding out to challenge Sauron at the Black Gates. He kept the black hose but exchanged the shirt for a red linen shirt smocked with corded leather braid. The soft boots were traded for heavier black boots fitted with steel plates engraved with seabirds' wings that protected the top of the foot, and steel greaves. He wore a full skirt of mail that was belted to the waist and put on a shirt of mail that was tightened with leather points, which laced through wide leather hems at the back, and with a leather belt buckled at the back of the neck (*left*). Fitted to this were pauldrons of steel and boiled leather edged in gold and engraved with elegant Gondorian motifs and feathers, and large steel-and-leather rerebraces fashioned to resemble the winged crown and seven stars of the king (*above right*). Boromir's vambraces completed the arm protection. Over this was worn a rich red velvet sleeveless robe, edged in gold and fitted with three silver buttons engraved with a star (*left*); then another robe, this time of black leather again edged in gold and fastened with silver clasps, which was emblazoned in silver with the Tree of Gondor surmounted by seven silver stars (*right*). A fine black cloak completed the outfit, attached to the outer robe by two gold and silver brooches.

It would not have suited a Ranger to carry a shield when traveling, and it was not something Aragorn ever employed in battle, although one was prepared for him when he donned his kingly armor prior to riding to the Black Gate to face Sauron. It was closer in shape to the shields of ancient Númenor; the wood was covered in black leather and edged and embossed in bronze with the Tree of Gondor, the seven stars and the winged crown that was the symbol of the king of Gondor alone.

Sauron

SAURON WAS A MAIA SPIRIT, the greatest of Morgoth's servants, and under his dominion Sauron came to be a powerful sorcerer. But when Thangorodrim was broken by the host of the Valar, and Morgoth was taken away in chains, Sauron fled from their judgment and hid himself in the dark. He eventually took for his realm the land of Mordor, for he saw that he could use the flames of Mount Doom as a crucible in which to forge his dark magics.

Sauron could not hope to dominate Middle-earth alone, so during the Second Age he gathered to him all the Orcs and other creatures that had survived the Valar's attack, and this host was mighty indeed. Sauron used them to overrun the greater part of Middle-earth, but he suffered great losses when his army was defeated by the Númenóreans and driven back

RIGHT *Map of Mordor recovered from Cirith Ungol.*
BELOW *Mount Doom was a dangerously unstable volcano.*

to Mordor. Hating all Men of Númenor for this humiliation, but fearing their military might, he devised a different strategy: after observing the Númenóreans' continual rise in power throughout the following 1,500 years, Sauron allowed himself to be taken prisoner and carried back to their island. Once there, however, he beguiled and seduced the king and his followers to a darker path, and this led to the almost complete destruction of this great race of Men. But Elendil and his sons escaped, even as Sauron fell into the abyss and his spirit was carried back on the winds to Mordor. After that Sauron had to assume the form of a burning man with blackened skin, and in this guise he was terrible to behold.

When Sauron was eventually able to take form again, centuries had passed, and he saw that Men and Elves had grown in number and power. He immediately launched an attack on Gondor, but he struck too soon, managing only to capture Minas Ithil before his force was repelled. This attack alerted the Free Peoples to his return, and the Last Alliance was formed; despite heavy losses on both sides, and the death of both Elendil and Gil-galad, whom he hated and feared above all others, Sauron was defeated and his spirit cast out of its body for a second time.

Almost a thousand years of the Third Age passed before Sauron was able to return from

the shadows. Without the One Ring, now lost to both sides, Sauron was much weakened, lacking the strength to assume bodily form; he feared to openly declare himself. Instead he sent the Witch-king, chief of his Nazgûl, to the northern realm of Angmar and here for five hundred years he made long and costly war against the Dúnedain of Arnor, almost completely eradicating the north kingdom before he was finally driven out by Elves from Rivendell and the Grey Havens. In the south, Easterlings and Haradrim made constant attacks against Gondor, gradually weakening the south kingdom from without; and as the line of kings failed Gondor, so it also became weakened from within.

All the while, Orcs continued to multiply in the Misty Mountains and in Mordor, overrunning the Dwarven kingdom of Moria and attacking the borders of Rohan and Gondor.

At this time Sauron returned to Mordor, rebuilt the Barad-dûr and began scouring Middle-earth for the One Ring, using the Nazgûl and spies in his efforts to recover the greater part of his power. By chance

Gollum came to Mordor and through torture revealed to Sauron the names "Baggins" and "Shire." In this way were the previously disregarded hobbit-folk drawn into the great war. But by driving the hobbit Ring-bearer from his hole, Sauron set in motion the events that would send the Ring almost within his grasp before it slipped through his fingers into the fires where it was unmade. His dreams of domination, which had been millennia in the planning, evaporated, his realm of Mordor crumbled and Sauron himself was sucked into the Void, from which there could be no return.

MACE

By all accounts, Sauron's mace was huge, nearly five feet long, made of black iron and fitted with six angular blades at its head. All along its surface was etched the same intaglio pattern present on Sauron's armor, which was said to have been inspired by a poison ivy-like weed that grew at the bottom of the bridge outside Minas Morgul. It is not known whether Sauron forged the weapon himself, nor whether he brought it with him out of the ruins of Thangorodrim. But there can be no doubt that he would have been closely involved in its making, for only someone as skilled in smithcraft as he could have forged such a mighty weapon. Its appearance on the battlefield would have greatly intimidated the Elves, who would have well recalled Grond, the Hammer of the Underworld, which was carried by Morgoth in the First Age and which claimed so many high-born of the Eldar.

DAGGER

Legend tells that Sauron made the One Ring by mixing his own blood with gold melted in his palm by the heat that burned within him. Sauron plunged a dagger into the center of the molten gold, creating a ring into which his blood flowed. Because of the great magic involved in the forging of this Ring, the dagger broke and was never seen again.

ARMOR

When Sauron took to the battlefield to face the Last Alliance of Elves and Men, he was already ancient in years, and his sable armor in some ways reflected the spirit that had been born when Middle-earth itself was still in its infancy. At that time Sauron allegedly still had bodily form and perhaps could have been harmed, so this may explain the presence of armor. The design was said to have been of an antiquity that was unique to Sauron alone. The intaglio decoration of a delicate twining poison contrasted with the brute ugliness of the spikes and blades, which stood out from his body like black thorns. The great helm was spiked like the horns of the Barad-dûr, and its long fluked sides gave it a shape eerily reminiscent of a horse's skull. Sauron armored himself in both mail and plate, all of which would have been superbly made, as he was a supremely skilled smith and would have demanded the very highest standards from those he directed to fashion his armor. It seems that there was a mail skirt and sleeves, but the rest of the body was covered in plate – collar, pauldrons, cuirass, rerebraces and vambraces, and cuisses, greaves and sabatons – that was a disharmonious combination of spikes, curves and straight lines. The silhouette created by all of this would have been alien and extremely intimidating.

One anonymous scribe speculated in his journal that the burning heat of Sauron's body had scorched his steel armor as black as his skin. He also wrote that when Sauron came into view it felt as though "a burning void had opened up on the battlefield." And it remains only speculation whether the armor and helm matched the form of the Dark Lord encased within, for no one alive during the War of the Ring ever saw his original form: to all, he was the Great Lidless Eye, burning in the void of his hunger and his hate.

The One Ring

OF ALL THE WEAPONS EVER TO EXIST in Middle-earth, none was more powerful or more deadly than the One Ring. Forged by Sauron deep with the fiery chambers of the Sammath Naur in Mount Doom, the Ring was impervious to all damage save that of the flames whence it came.

To make it a thing of surpassing power, Sauron poured his cruelty, his malice and his will to dominate all life into the Ring; the greater part of his power went into it, so much so that it became almost a living thing and could exert its own desires upon the wearer. There was almost no one in Middle-earth who could resist its power. The Red Book of Westmarch tells how even Galadriel, the oldest and most powerful Elf in all of Middle-earth, struggled to deny it, and Saruman, chief of the order of Istari, was corrupted by his desire to possess it.

The One Ring was, unlike all the other Rings of Power, a plain gold band, but it bore an inscription written by Sauron in a special Black Speech version of the Elven Tengwar lettering:

Ash nazg durbatulûk, ash nazg gimbatul,
Ash nazg thrakatulûk, agh burzum ishi krimpatul.

These words were spoken by Sauron when he forged the Ring and are translated as:

One Ring to rule them all, One Ring to find them,
One Ring to bring them all and in the darkness bind them.

The inscription, which could be seen only when the Ring was heated, was designed to ensnare the other Rings of Power.

The Red Book makes it clear that the Ring used and devoured its wearers, stretching out their lives to an unbearable length while it fed on their lives. This was highlighted by what happened when the wearer put on the Ring; he would disappear completely. Although useful in the short term it boded very ill for the future, giving an all too clear indication of what would eventually come to pass.

Such was the magnitude of evil contained within this tiny object that there was no possibility of using it for good; any noble deeds attempted through it would soon come to ruin, and likely it would find its way back to its master and creator, Sauron. There was only one possible course of action to take: to destroy it, to take it back into Mordor and cast it into the flames at the Crack of Doom.

After much suffering and loss, Frodo Baggins of the Shire was able to do this. The unmaking of the One Ring destroyed Sauron's greatest weapon, along with the greater part of him and all his most powerful creatures. And Sauron's destruction allowed the Return of the King and the beginning of the Fourth Age, an age of peace.

Glossary of Terms

ARMOR

HEAD

Aventail A "curtain" of mail hanging from the back of the *helmet* to protect the back and sides of the neck. This would be constructed in the same way as a *hauberk*. Gimli the Dwarf had an aventail made of small scales fixed to the back of his *sallet*.

Barbut Conical, open-faced helmet, whose sides and back extended down to protect the neck. The helmets worn by Gondorian soldiers were a form of barbut.

Coif Cap or hood that protected the head. Typically it would be padded and quilted, sometimes made of leather, and would often be worn under a mail hood, which could be referred to then as a mail coif. Men of lesser rank in the Rohan army would have had these if they could not afford a plate or plate-and-leather helmet. Mail coifs were also worn by Elven soldiers during the Last Alliance.

Crest A helmet could be fitted with a decorative device for identification purposes. A crest could also have practical protective benefits, depending on what it was made from. The metal "crescent blades" on Elven helmets would be of some use in deflecting blows, and even a simple horsehair crest affixed to the top of a helmet could bind an enemy's weapon or at least confuse his aim.

Helmet Most of the helmets worn during the War of the Ring were open-faced types, though there were notable exceptions, such as those worn by the Uruk-hai and the Easterlings. A helmet might have integral protection for the cheeks, face and back of the neck (Elven helmets were good examples) or they might have separate pieces that served the same purpose, such as the plates protecting the eyes of the Rohan Royal Guard. Helmets fitted with separate visors (face-plates) were much more common among the Orcs. A helmet that completely enclosed the head was known as a helm.

Sallet A helmet that protected the head, usually from below the ears and upward, and extended at the back to a tail; it could be either open-faced or fully enclosed with a slit through which to see. This enclosed sallet was worn by the Uruk-hai sappers.

Skull The main part of a helmet.

Standard A stiff collar of mail that protected the neck; standards were usually reinforced with leather and were secured with leather points.

TORSO

Aketon A quilted tunic worn under a *hauberk* or plate armor; quilted vertically, its padding would diffuse the impact from a weapon such as an axe or a hacking blow from a sword and minimize the discomfort of wearing metal next to skin. See also *gambeson*.

Backplate Plate-armor protection for the back; the second principal element of a *cuirass*, which was strapped to a *breastplate*.

Breastplate Plate-armor protection for the chest and stomach; the principal piece in a *cuirass*, which was attached to a *backplate* using *leathers*.

Cuirass The entire defense protecting the torso. A plate cuirass usually comprised a *breastplate*, *backplate*, *fauld* and *culet*. These would be attached together using *points* or *leathers*.

Culet Plate defense below the *backplate*.

Fauld Hooped skirt of interlinked lames protecting the lower abdomen, which was worn below the *breastplate*. A pair of plate *tassets* was sometimes attached to the lower half of the fauld to give further protection.

Gambeson A quilted tunic worn over a *hauberk* or plate armor; its padding would diffuse the impact of a weapon's blow. See also *aketon*.

Hauberk A complete shirt made of scale or chain-mail worn beneath other armor, if it was available. In the War of the Ring hauberks were variously sleeveless or sleeved to the wrist, elbow or bicep. Mail was generally constructed from joined circular or oval-shaped metal rings, riveted, welded or simply butted together to form a flexible layer of protection. Hauberks were occasionally edged with leather, with holes punched into these hems, making it easier to put on and remove the hauberk, and also allowing it to be firmly laced to the body using *leathers* or *points*.

Jerkin A sleeveless tunic, usually made of leather. Sleeves of leather or mail could be attached using points, if desired, and removed when the weather was warmer or the threat of attack unlikely.

Lame A strip of steel that provided articulated protection for a soldier, usually around his joints. Lames were either riveted together or linked using *points*. See *pauldron, sabatons*.

Leathers Leather straps used to join two pieces of armor; they would pass through holes that had been made in the plate or mail and then be secured with small buckles.

Plackart Plate armor that protected the stomach; examples were recovered on the battlefield from fallen Orcs, although it is not known whether the armor they were wearing as plackarts was originally intended for that purpose.

Point A lace used to attach smaller pieces of armor together and to tie up clothing. Points could be made from flax, buckskin or twine.

Tabard A loose surcoat, usually open at the sides, that was put on over the head and worn outside the armor; it was used to display the wearer's heraldic emblems (hence "coat of arms").

ARM

Couter Curved plate that covered the elbow and also bridged the gap between the *rerebrace* and *vambrace*.

Gauntlet A covering for the hand and usually the lower forearm; usually a heavy leather glove with a wrist cuff but sometimes covered with articulated plates or mail. Gauntlets were often secured by small leather straps that would be tightened on the wrist by using the small metal buckle.

Glove The majority of fighting men would have worn leather gloves, both to aid their grip on the weapon when everything was covered in blood and to protect themselves from cuts and bruising. When in combat it was inevitable that their hands would come into contact with sharp edges, claws or even teeth, and so wearing gloves helped reduce the risk of infection. On the battlefield the warrior might be several days' journey away from a healer, so gloves sometimes made the difference between life and death.

Haute-piece Curved flange on the top of a *pauldron* that extended upward to protect the side of the neck from attack by sword or axe. See also *stop-rib*.

Manifer Large metal *gauntlet* for the left hand, which could also be worn over an ordinary gauntlet. The manifers worn by the Uruk-hai pikesmen were further adorned with a coronel, a small crown of points similar to those seen on a morning star.

Pauldron Curved plate or plates that protected the shoulder joint against attack from all directions. A pauldron could be just one large, single plate, or it could be composed of a number of overlapping, articulated *lames*. In either case the entire unit would still be referred to as a pauldron. The top of a pauldron would often feature a *haute-piece* or have a *stop-rib* riveted to it, in order to protect the neck from a sideways attack.

Rerebrace Curved or cylindrical plate or plates that covered the upper arm.

Sleeve In many instances during the War of the Ring soldiers had no more substantial arm defense than a mail sleeve. Wealthier soldiers wore a mail sleeve beneath other arm defenses so it could protect the otherwise exposed gaps. A mail sleeve could be full length or could end at the wrist, the elbow, or be even shorter. It usually formed part of the *hauberk* but could also be attached to a leather *jerkin*.

Stop-rib Raised strip of steel that was welded to the top of a *pauldron* in order to deflect blows away from the neck. See also *haute-piece*.

Vambrace Curved or completely cylindrical plate that covered the forearm. Vambraces made specifically to protect an archer's arm from the slap of the released bowstring were called bracers. Vambraces of boiled leather were typically worn over mail sleeves, although two-layer vambraces like those worn by Rangers were usually sufficient to ward off all but the most serious blows.

LEG

Cuisse Curved or cylindrical plate protecting the thighs.

Greaves Curved or cylindrical plates protecting the shins and calves.

Hose Most warriors usually wore their ordinary hose, or leggings, into combat, and over them was placed any armor such as a mail skirt and *greaves*. Gondorian hose had mail attached to the legs from the knees down. Because of the need to march for long distances, an infantryman generally wore little more than steel or leather greaves in order to lessen the weight on his legs.

Poleyn A curved plate or plates that protected the knee joint and also bridged the gap between the upper and lower leg defenses.

Rumpguard Plate protecting the buttocks that was attached to the *culet*.

Sabatons Armoured boots comprised of articulated *lames* that allowed the foot to flex when walking.

Skirt Fully enclosing curtain of armor that protected the legs. Skirts were made of mail or scale and, because of their weight, were belted at the waist.

Tall Boots Often, heavy leather boots were worn as an alternative or supplement to *greaves*. Depending on their construction, they may have had little value in stopping blades. However, they still served a protective function, particularly for mounted warriors, by preventing the rider's legs from chafing against the horse's flank and also protecting against cuts and scrapes from thistles, branches and other hazards encountered when riding.

Tasset Small piece of plate armor that hung from the *fauld*, giving further protection to the hips, particularly in the case of mounted warriors, who would need additional hip protection. Tassets could be attached to the fauld by either *leathers* or rivets, or even, when worn below a breast- or backplate, by a separate belt.

Shield

Although a defensive piece of armor, a shield could also be used offensively to punch, ram or even stab an enemy. Shields were generally made of wood, leather or metal, depending on the relative availability of these resources. Wooden shields were made from thin planks, nailed together or glued; then another layer of planks would be added, running in a different direction from the first so that the layers of ply would be built up. A leather covering would often be added, which would reinforce the shield as well as serve as a useful waterproofing device against the hostile elements. If a shield had a boss, the domed structure in the center to protect the hand from blows, it was nearly always made of metal, with a metal bar on the inside that served as a handgrip. The main disadvantage to the boss was that a blow to the side of the shield could cause it to turn in the warrior's hand, as all stability was dependent on the strength in his wrist. Such a blow could easily continue into and through the warrior. As an alternative to a boss, some shields had a handgrip and enarmes, or carrying straps; when the shield was held using these, it would lie along the flat of the forearm so that any blow was absorbed and diffused rather than taken directly. A shield would often have a guige, a longer strap so that it could be slung over the warrior's shoulder or from his saddle when traveling.

WEAPONS

Arming sword A soldier's principal fighting sword; it was nearly always a single-handed weapon. A sword with a long handgrip that allowed it to be wielded either one- or two-handed was known as a hand-and-a-half, or bastard, sword.

Arrow Missile that was fired from a *bow*. Arrows would be made of wood or similar materials that were light and could be fashioned into a straight length; they were then stained or painted to keep out moisture and prevent warping. The arrow would be *nocked* at the back so that it could fit over the string, and would feature a weighted head of some hard substance that would be the striking point: these would range from finely shaped metal heads, as used by the Elves, Gondorians and Rohan, to flint, obsidian, ivory or bone. To keep the arrow on a straight course when in flight, it would be fledged with a rigid material at the back, ideally feathers – turkey, goose, swan or perhaps crow – because they were the lightest and most durable, but any number of other materials have been found: fur, leather and even hair taken from an enemy beard or scalp. Orcs would have been unconcerned about the material used as they would expect to get through a lot of arrows in their indiscriminate firing. For a long-standing battle such as that fought at Dagorlad by the Last Alliance, it is likely there would have been a supply train equipped with extra arrows and runners who would carry bundles up to where they were needed on the field. The supply train would also have carried food and medical supplies.

Axe A medium- or long-handled weapon with a metal head usually sharpened along one edge. The difference between an axe and a sword is that a sword was used for cutting, slashing and thrusting, whereas an axe was made for impact and cleaving. Axes varied in design, with some featuring large double-bladed heads; these were known as battle axes and because of their weight needed to be wielded with both hands. The force generated by the use of both arms to swing it, coupled with the weight of the axe head, meant that the impact alone was enough to cause great damage; combined with the cutting edge of the blade, such a blow meant almost certain death. When an axe was wielded one-handed the warrior usually carried a shield on his other arm, alternately hacking with the axe and raising the shield. Axes were generally favored by Dwarves and by strong warriors possessed of a less sophisticated fighting style, such as the Rohan. Smaller versions of the one-handed axe would be used as throwing axes; these would have a longer handle and a relatively smaller head; their blade would curve up and in toward the shaft, creating a larger mass of metal farther away from the throwing hand and from the shaft, which would help rotate the axe through the air on its way to the target. As armor improved, it got to the point that a one-handed sword was almost ineffective against it, but an axe was still able to smash or cut through. (A sword was very good against lightly armored or unarmored people, as it is a very maneuverable weapon, but when the enemy is wearing heavy armor, it could be very hard to find a weak point. In this situation axes and maces excelled; they were able to cut through the armor, and even if they didn't they generated so much impact at the point where they struck that they damaged the enemy without having to break through the armor itself.)

Bodkin A long arrowhead, without barbs, which was used for hunting and piercing armor. A bodkin could also be a small dagger, often carried in a sheath fixed to a sword scabbard, such as that carried by Aragorn on his Ranger sword.

Bolt Missile fired from a *crossbow*; the metal-tipped bolt was thicker than an *arrow* and would therefore be more effective at punching through an enemy's armor.

Because of the power and accuracy of the crossbow, the bolt did not need to be as sophisticated as the arrow: its flights were generally only of leather or iron.

Bow Range weapon that utilizes the force generated by bending the stave of the bow to then propel the missile by means of a string fixed under tension to the stave. Bows were either short or long: a longbow was usually made from a single piece of wood, tapered in the limbs so that it bowed when the string was attached; a shortbow was more likely to be laminated or composite, that is, either built up from different layers of wood that were glued together or formed from a combination of wood and other materials such as horn. A shortbow was often recurved, shaped so that it curved away from the string, which meant that when the string was fitted the stave had to be bent back much farther – and therefore was under much greater tension – than with a longbow, in order to introduce as much power as possible into its smaller size. Third Age bows did not have an arrow rest, so the bow was tilted to keep the arrow steady in the V created by the stave and the hand.

Broad-head A wide, barbed arrowhead with long cutting edges. Used principally for hunting larger prey, it was highly effective on the battlefield.

Chape A metal cap that fitted over the end of the *scabbard* to protect it and the sword tip, which the chape encased.

Crossbow Mechanical version of the *bow*, which eschewed the physical capabilities and subtleties of the human physique in favor of the consistency of the machine. Whereas the range and accuracy of a bow were entirely dependent on the arm and aim of the bowman, a crossbow could be repeatedly fired to the same point as long as the strength of the crossbowman held out; as these infernal weapons were created by Saruman for his Uruk-hai, that would have been a very long time indeed.

Cross-guard Metal cross-piece that fitted over the *tang* and butted up to the *ricasso*. The cross-guard stopped the enemy sword from sliding past the ricasso and into the wielder's sword hand, and prevented the hand sliding along the blade when he thrust into his foe; it also served as a buttress for the sword hand to further strengthen the grip. The shape of the middle part of the cross-guard was normally matched by the shape of the *locket* and mouth, so that the sword and *scabbard* fitted snugly together, creating a water-resistant seal. It was also known as a guard, especially when the design was of a more irregular shape. See *Men of Rohan*.

Falchion A single-edged sword that was used like a cleaver. This was the principal weapon of the Uruk-hai swordsmen.

Gisarme A long staff weapon that had at its tip a curved axe head whose lower point was attached to the haft. This was the primary weapon carried by Uruk-hai pikesmen.

Glaive A long spearlike weapon with a curved, single-edged blade at its end. The most famous example of this type of weapon was Aiglos, the legendary spear belonging to Gil-galad, high king of the Noldor.

Halberd A staff weapon with a spike at the top and an axe blade backed by a hammer or spike; some also featured a spike at the bottom. A versatile weapon, it allowed the warrior to defend or attack from almost any direction. This was the primary weapon of the Easterlings. Also known as a polearm or poleaxe, especially if the blade was backed with a hammer.

Handgrip Wooden cylinder that was hollowed so that it could be fitted over the *tang* between the *cross-guard* and *pommel*. To improve the grip of the sword, the handgrip was wrapped in cords of twine or leather that were glued to it; on richer weapons it would be swaged with bronze rings that were in turn encased in leather. Also known as a hilt.

Lance A long spear used when on horseback; the lance was sturdier than an ordinary spear so, although it couldn't be thrown as far, its additional weight made it a very effective and deadly weapon against armored opponents.

Locket A circular metal plate that was fitted around the mouth of a *scabbard* to protect the wood and leather from wear caused by repeated drawing of the sword. The locket and the scabbard's mouth would normally be the same shape as the middle part of the *cross-guard*, so that the sword would fit flush to the scabbard, preventing any rain from getting inside the scabbard and onto the blade.

Mace A heavy club fitted with various types of weapons at its end, ranging from an unadorned square or rounded head, a spiked metal ball – if this was fitted to a chain it was known as a morning-star. Perhaps the finest example of a mace ever seen in Middle-earth was also the most infamous, for Sauron himself wielded it when he stepped forth to face the Last Alliance of Elves and Men.

Nock A grooved piece of wood, either at each end of a *bow* or the back of an *arrow*, into which was placed the string of the bow. The nock on an arrow was often reinforced by inserting a small piece of bone, flint or other hard substance at the bottom of the groove; this was done so that – especially with Elven and Gondorian longbows – the enormous force of a released bowstring did not just continue through the arrow, splitting it down the middle.

Pike A long spear carried by infantry; the pikes carried by the Uruk-hai were actually closer in appearance to a *gisarme* than a pike.

Pommel The weighted end of a sword hilt, used to counterbalance the blade. The pommel was hollowed so that it could fit over the *tang*; it was secured by pinging over the exposed tip of the tang. The balance of a sword was crucial. If the blade was too heavy, the swordsman would become tired and the impact of his blows would lessen; if the pommel was too heavy, not enough of the force of the swing would be transferred into the blade. A long sword, such as Narsil or Glamdring, tended to also have a long, scent-bottle-shaped pommel.

Quiver A long narrow case used to carry *arrows*. Quivers were usually made from wood or leather, or a combination of both, so as to keep the weight that a bowman carried as light as possible. Rohan quivers had an internal drawstring canvas bag that could be pulled up and over their arrows, protecting them from the rain when not in use but more importantly preventing them from bouncing out of the quiver when the bowman was riding. When he was part of a defensive line on the rampart, defending against a siege such as at Helm's Deep or Minas Tirith, the supply of arrows in his quiver would have been bolstered by barrels full of extra arrows placed at intervals along the battlement. If the bowman was part of an advancing force he would have looked to pick up arrows as he moved through the bodies of the slain.

Ricasso The top section of the sword blade, which was usually left blunt, as warriors would often place their index finger in front of the *cross-guard*. This action changed the position of the sword in relation to the arm so that it extended in the same direction as the arm, rather than being at right angles, which was the usual position when it was gripped in the fist. The advantage to this position was that it allowed the warrior to thrust more effectively at his armored opponent; the disadvantage was that it left the finger extremely vulnerable, so a protective finger ring was fitted to the cross-guard. See *Nazgûl*.

Scabbard Sheath that protected the sword when not in use; it would usually be made of wood and covered in leather. For a sword of greater importance or ceremonial use, such as Denethor's, the scabbard was often adorned in metal or even decorated with gems. The mouth of the scabbard was protected with a metal *locket*, and the tip with a *chape*. The sword would spend almost all of its life in the scabbard, so the sword and scabbard were considered a unit. There was also the belt and suspension system; this would have varied among cultures, and also would have been dictated by the length of the sword, the cultural fighting style and the individual preference of the swordsman. Those with a shorter sword or desiring a quicker draw would have worn their sword at an angle away from the body; those with longer swords, such as the Númenóreans, had to have theirs hanging straight down. The Elves wore theirs across their backs, drawing the sword with their pommel hand, then adding the guard hand at the same time as they brought it forward in a downward-sweeping arc. The wooden core of a typical scabbard tended to be fragile, and scabbards often became broken in use. The metal fittings would be taken off the old scabbard to make a new one, and if the sword had been handed down to a new owner he might also add his own embellishments, such as changing the color of the leather covering.

Tang The continuation of a sword blade as it passed through into the hilt.

Hige sceal þe heardra, heorte þe cenre,
Mod sceal þe mare þe ure maegen lytlað